CLASSICAL QUILLS I

STUDENT TEXT

EILEEN CUNNINGHAM

Edited by Amy Alexander Carmichael

Lochinvar Press
Wichita, KS

Text Copyright © 2016 Eileen Cunningham and Amy Alexander Carmichael

ISBN: 978-0692431740

All rights reserved.

To the community of the

Classical School of Wichita

Wichita, Kansas

Table of Contents

Chapter 1: Fable 1

Chapter 2: Description 11

Chapter 3: Narrative 25

Chapter 4: Writing a Good Paragraph 43

Chapter 5: Proverb and Chreia 59

Chapter 6: Encomium and Invective 79

Chapter 7: Refutation and Confirmation 93

Chapter 8: Commonplace 117

Chapter 9: Comparison 125

Chapter 10: Speech-in-Character 135

INTRODUCTION

Definition of *Progymnasmata*

The Greek word *progymnasmata* (pro-goom-NAHZ-ma-tuh) is composed of the prefix *pro- (fore, pre-)* and the root *–gymnas (exercise)*. Together, they are rendered in English as the early or preliminary exercises. To be specific, they are the exercises rhetoric teachers considered foundational to the study of rhetoric. A student was expected to have mastered them before beginning actual rhetoric classes.

History of the Progymnasmata

The earliest mention of the progymnasmata can be found in a rhetorical handbook dated to the fourth century BC. By the first century AD, separate handbooks for the progymnasmata were written and circulated. Perhaps the most famous handbooks were written by Hermogenes of Tarsus in the second century AD and the great orator Aphthonius in the fourth century AD.[1]

Aphthonius included fourteen exercises in his handbook:

Fable (*Mythos*)	Commonplace (*Koinos topos*)
Narrative (*Diêgêma*)	Encomium (*Enkōmion*)
Description (*Ekphrasis*)	Invective (*Psogos*)
Proverb (*Gnōmê*)	Comparison (*Synkrisis*)
Anecdote (*Chreia*)	Speech in Character (*Prosōpopoeia*)

Refutation (*Anaskeuê*) Thesis (*Thesis*)
Confirmation (*Kataskeuê*) Legislation (*Nomos*)

In our earlier books, *Writing the Classical Way I* and *II*, we included all fourteen of the elements and introduced all approaches for each. But when it was decided to introduce classical composition to students in the last two years of grammar school (fifth and sixth grades), we combined similar elements of the progymnasmata together and reduced the number of approaches, fitting *Classical Quills I* and *II* more suitably to the age group. Thus, Proverb and Chreia appear together as do Refutation/Confirmation and Encomium/Invective. *Classical Quills I* has been further abridged by omitting the last two elements, Thesis and Law.

A chapter entitled "Writing a Good Paragraph" has also been included so that students can learn to present material deductively, moving from general to specific, which is the foundational pattern of discourse among the English-speaking peoples.

Values-Based Education

The ideal of a Greek education was to produce "a good man speaking well." First the progymnasmata and then the study of rhetoric certainly assist the student to speak (or write) well, but the first part of the motto must not be forgotten: classical education is equally concerned with teaching students to think morally and ethically. This focus may be one of the main reasons why the Judeo-Christian world was able to adopt Greco-Roman education so readily: it cultivated virtue.

Nowhere is this emphasis more clear than in the progymnasmata itself. Every one of the elements—from Fable to Law—asks students to address issues of morality and, in a Christian context, to hold everything up to the standards of moral and ethical conduct set out in Scripture.

This feature of education, designed by pagan Greeks and Romans, has been nearly abandoned in many public schools in the United States today, but the desire of many to re-institute what we now call *values-based education* finds satisfaction in the routine elements of the progymnasmata. For this reason, if for no other, Christian schools should introduce the progymnasmata to children at the earliest possible stage so that they can begin to craft their responses to the issues facing our culture in ways compatible with their faith.

Grammar, Logic, and Rhetoric Stages in *Classical Quills*

Each chapter begins with definitions and examples. These constitute the Grammar Stage.

Definitions and examples are followed by "Think It Through" questions, where students apply the concepts to their own experience. Model compositions come next, followed by student analysis of the model. These constitute the Logic stage.

Finally, students are asked to explore ways to use the element to address issues within their own experience. The chapter ends with an original composition on a debatable issue. These constitute the Rhetoric stage.

A Note on Readiness

In his text *Institutes of Oratory*, Quintilian, a Roman rhetorician of the first century AD, addressed the issue of age-appropriateness, saying: "I think that the question when a boy ought to be sent to the teacher of rhetoric is best decided by the answer, when he shall be qualified."[2] Today chronological age governs school progress more than mental readiness, yet teachers still must make decisions everyday as to whether students are ready for X or Y. Therefore, within the context of the individual classroom, the teacher may find that there are some students who are not ready to engage the later elements—such as Refutation/Confirmation, Thesis, and Law. This is not a failure of the teacher or the student. This is simply the nature of growth. For this reason, the classroom teacher or homeschooling parent is encouraged to use discretion.

The models in these later chapters have been selected with a nod toward chronological age. Models for both volumes are pulled from great works of children's literature such as *Alice in Wonderland*, *Oliver Twist*, *The Adventures of Huckleberry Finn*, and *Peter Pan*. Issues for discussion and debate are related to the life experience of the age group—defending a classmate wrongly accused of cheating (Refutation), spurning bad language (Commonplace), explaining why Abraham Lincoln was a great man (Encomium). It is believed students will naturally have strong feelings about such issues, and what remains is for the teacher to give the students the tools they need to help them articulate their ideas in a clear-headed manner.

We are well advised to use common sense in order to present the progymnasmata in a way that challenges but does not frustrate students. For those more difficult exercises in the later chapters, perhaps guided writing, using laptop projectors or—what students sometimes prefer—a class "scribe" at the board, should supersede the assignment of individual compositions written alone as homework. Students who are ready to fly solo, so to speak, should also be encouraged to do so. It is the teacher's call.

The production of a Scope and Sequence within the context of the individual school would also provide teachers with some guidance in these matters.

Scripture References in *Classical Quills*

Unless otherwise specified, the English Standard Version of the Bible has been used throughout *Classical Quills I* and *II*.

Acknowledgements

We wish to thank the Classical School of Wichita's board, administration, faculty, parents, and students for supporting us in this project. Special thanks to teachers Kris Darrah and Michelle Young and to student Hannah M. for testing the materials. Their feedback has encouraged us and improved the materials greatly. Any errors that might remain are, of course, our own. We are committed to producing materials of a quality which honors our Lord and Savior, Jesus Christ: "Whatever you do, work heartily, as for the Lord and not for men, knowing that from the Lord you will receive the inheritance as your reward. You are serving the Lord Christ" (Col. 3:23–24). In order to improve the work to achieve the highest standard, we welcome input from all who use or have an interest in these materials.

Contact Information

Please feel free to contact us with questions, observations, or suggestions at writingtheclassicalway@gmail.com.

FABLE

Chapter 1

Introduction

> A Shepherd-boy, who watched a flock of sheep near a village, brought out the villagers three or four times by crying out, "Wolf! Wolf!" and when his neighbors came to help him, laughed at them for their pains. The Wolf, however, did truly come at last. The Shepherd-boy, now really alarmed, shouted in an agony of terror: "Pray, do come and help me; the Wolf is killing the sheep"; but no one paid any heed to his cries, nor rendered any assistance. The Wolf, having no cause of fear, at his leisure lacerated or destroyed the whole flock.
>
> There is no believing a liar, even when he speaks the truth.[3]

Tales like "The Boy Who Cried Wolf" are what we call *fables*. The most famous writer of fables was probably Aesop, who dwelt in ancient Greece. In ancient Greece and Rome, parents and teachers would use fables to teach children proper behavior. For example, "The Boy Who Cried Wolf" teaches children why lying is not good behavior.

However, the ancients did not use fables just for the instruction of children. Their famous orators would use fables to help persuade decision makers one way or the other. For example, one of Aesop's fables well known in Greece was that of "The Lion's Share." It went this way:

The Lion's Share
By Aesop

The Lion went once a-hunting along with the Fox, the Jackal, and the Wolf. They hunted and they hunted till at last they surprised a Stag, and soon took its life. Then came the question how the spoil should be divided. "Quarter me this Stag," roared the Lion; so the other animals skinned it and cut it into four parts. Then the Lion took his stand in front of the carcass and pronounced judgment: "The first quarter is for me in my capacity as King of Beasts; the second is mine as arbiter; another share comes to me for my part in the chase; and as for the fourth quarter—well, as for that, I should like to see which of you will dare to lay a paw upon it."[4]

The famous philosopher Socrates, a citizen of Athens, once used this fable in a speech in which he charged that all the gold of Greece—and all in the rest of the world as well—had been going to Sparta as the spoils of war. Sparta, like the Lion, was getting richer while other Greek cities and the rest of the world, like the Fox, the Jackal, and the Wolf, were getting poorer. In recounting this fable, Socrates was trying to persuade the Athenians to stand up to their old rival, the Spartans. So, here we see a famous philosopher using a child's fable to make an important speech in the Athenian Senate!

The ancient Greeks were not the only people to write fables. Almost every culture has fables, and we see them also in Jewish literature (the Old Testament) and in the parables of Jesus in the New Testament.

Definition and Purpose of a Fable

A fable is a very short story that could be used in one of these ways:

1. Parents and teachers can use fables to teach children proper behavior.

2. Senators and other public speakers can use fables to help people understand a particular problem better.

3. Leaders might use fables to persuade others to a certain course of action.

THINK IT THROUGH: One of Aesop's most famous fables is the one called "The Tortoise and the Hare." Briefly summarize that fable and indicate what you think the moral lesson of the fable is. Have you ever seen a real-life situation where someone needed to be reminded of the Tortoise and the Hare? Explain that information for your classmates.

Characteristics of the Fable

1. **Characters:** The characters in a fable can be people, animals, or even things (such as trees or rivers). In some fables, there might be a mixture of two or more character types.

   THINK IT THROUGH: Can you think of any Bible parables that include animals that speak? How about features of nature such as trees or clouds?

2. **Names:** The characters normally do not have names such as "Tully" or "Wally the Wolf." Rather, as we see above, they are just called "Shepherd Boy" or "Wolf."

   THINK IT THROUGH: Look again at the fables we have been talking about and notice the use of capitalization. Why do you think writers of fables often capitalize these common nouns?

3. **Moral:** The fable should end with a moral to be learned. It normally appears at the end of the fable.

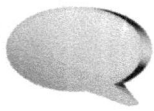 **THINK IT THROUGH:** What would you write as the moral to "The Lion's Share"?

EXERCISE 1.1: Examining a Fable

 Directions: Please read the fables below and answer the questions that follow.

The Fly and the Bald Man

A Fly bit the bare head of a Bald Man who, endeavoring to destroy it, gave himself a heavy slap. Escaping, the Fly said mockingly, "You who have wished to revenge, even with death, the Prick of a tiny insect, see what you have done to yourself to add insult to injury?" The Bald Man replied, "I can easily make peace with myself, because I know there was no intention to hurt. But you, an ill-favored and contemptible insect who delights in sucking human blood, I wish that I could have killed you even if I had incurred a heavier penalty."

Moral: "Revenge will hurt the avenger."[5]

Questions:

1. Re-tell the story in one or two sentences.

2. Are the characters humans, animals, objects, or a mixture?

3. What is the moral to the fable?

4. Where is the moral located?

Jesus' Parable of the Lost Sheep
Luke 15:4-7

⁴ "What man of you, having a hundred sheep, if he has lost one of them, does not leave the ninety-nine in the open country, and go after the one that is lost, until he finds it? ⁵ And when he has found it, he lays it on his shoulders, rejoicing. ⁶ And when he comes home, he calls together his friends and his neighbors, saying to them, 'Rejoice with me, for I have found my sheep that was lost.' ⁷ Just so, I tell you, there will be more joy in heaven over one sinner who repents than over ninety-nine righteous persons who need no repentance."

1. In one or two sentences, summarize the story of "The Parable of the Lost Sheep."

2. What kind of characters are in this story: human, animal, objects, or a mixture?

3. In which verse do we find the moral?

4. In your own words, write the moral of the fable.

The Expanded Fable

Sometimes writers will take a familiar fable of just three or four sentences and expand it into a longer story. To do this, they add dialogue and descriptive detail not found in the original. In fact, sometimes filmmakers will even create a movie out of a fable or parable. One example is the 2014 movie entitled *A Long Way Off* (PG), which is a modern re-telling of the parable of the Prodigal Son. The parable, which can be found in the Gospel of Luke, is told in only twenty-two verses (about 500 words, depending on the translation). However, the screenwriter, John Macy, turned this powerful story into a movie that is one hour and forty minutes long.

Word Choice in an Expanded Fable

The words of a fable are normally quite simple. However, when converting a short fable into an expanded version, a writer should follow the fundamental skill of a storyteller: "Show, don't tell!" This means that a good writer chooses precise words rather than vague words.

For example, the original fable might read as follows:

> "The Hare often *walked* before the other animals and *told* them that he could run faster than any of them."

> But students who expand the fable would want to do more than just report what the Hare said in such a flat way. They might want to choose a word that would help show the conceited way the Hare behaves and speaks to others, thus:

> "The Hare would often *strut* before the other animals and *boast*, "I could beat anyone of you, on any day, in any place!"

What Do We See Here?

1. Notice that in the original statement, we read that the Hare liked to *walk* in front of the other animals. However, in the expanded version, what more specific verb is used in place of *walk*?

   Why is this a better choice?

2. In the original version, we read that the Hare often *told* the other animals something. But in the expanded version, what synonym is used for *tell*?

   Why is this a better word choice?

3. In the original statement, the author simply summarizes what the Hare said, but in the expanded version, we see exactly what he said. Copy the Hare's exact words in this space:

EXERCISE 1.2: Examining an Expanded Fable

Directions: Below you will see a very short fable followed by an expanded version. Please read both versions and then answer the questions that follow.

The Swimming Boy
By Aesop
(Short Version)

A boy swimming in a river was in danger of being drowned. He called out to a passing traveler for help, but instead of holding out a helping hand, the man stood by unworried and scolded the boy for his bad judgment. "Oh, sir!" cried the youth. "Please help me now and scold me afterwards."[6]

Moral: Counsel without help is useless.

The Swimming Boy (Expanded Version)
By Aesop

(1) One day a boy was all alone and a bit bored as he walked about in the countryside. (2) He thought to himself, "The sun is shining and the wind is not blowing. (3) What a perfect day, but I don't have anyone to share it with." (4) Rounding a turn in the lane, the boy noticed a lovely river flowing in front of him. (5) The rays of the sun glanced off the ripples as the water flowed calmly past him. (6) "I think I'm just going to hop in this river and have a little swim," he said to himself. (7) It will make the time pass much more pleasantly." (8) And so he popped off his shoes and jumped in. (9) He splashed about this way and that, and dived under the water to see if he could observe a fish at play. (10) He took a pebble from the bank and threw it into the middle of the river. Then swam to the spot and dived down to search for it. (11) He swam from bank to bank several times, just to see if he could improve his speed each time. (12) Such fun was the boy having that he did not notice the dark clouds rolling in to hide the lovely blue sky. (13) Nor did he notice that the wind had started to blow, turning the lovely ripples in the river into churning waves. (14) "I'd better get home," he thought to himself. (15) But as he started to swim from the far side of the river to the bank where he had left his shoes, he was much too tuckered out to cover the distance. (16) He struggled and gasped for air as the water seemed to be pulling him down. (17) This went on for a while until suddenly the boy noticed a traveler passing by on the same road which he himself had been following. (18) He called to the traveler, "Help! Help!" (19) Hearing the cry, the traveler stopped in the road, put his hands on his hips, and yelled, "Lad, you were foolish to get yourself into the middle of that river on a stormy day!" (20) "But help me! Please, help me!" the boy hollered back, but the man only replied, "Young man, you've really gotten yourself into a pickle. Didn't your parents ever teach you that you should think before you act?" (21) By now the boy was desperate. (22) Each time he opened his mouth to implore the traveler for help, water would rush in, and he would choke and gag and thrash about all the more. (23) Finally, he mustered up all the strength in him and moved his arms like the fins of a fish in order to tread water just long enough to shout to the traveler, "Help me get out now! I'll take your scolding later!"

Moral: "Counsel without help is useless."

Questions:

1. In your own words, summarize the fable of "The Swimming Boy."

2. What is the moral of "The Swimming Boy"?

3. With a highlighter, highlight all the dialogue that was added in the expanded version of the fable, including both speech and thoughts. The first one is done for you as an example.

4. As the boy begins to speak to the traveler, the writer has selected verbs that can be used to introduce the characters' words. If the writer used the tags *the boy said* and *the traveler said* every time, the fable would be a bit weak. In the space provided, write down all the stronger verbs that mean about the same thing as *say*? The first one is done for you as an example.

Sentence 18: *called*

Sentence 19: _____

Sentence 20: _____ and _____

Sentence 23: _____

EXERCISE 1.3: Expanding a Fable with Your Classmates

Directions: Project the following fable on the board. As a class, indicate places where dialogue and description could be added. Then, have one class member serve as a scribe to write on the board an expanded fable dictated by the class members.

The Hen and the Golden Eggs

A cottager and his wife had a Hen that laid a golden egg every day. They supposed that the Hen must contain a great lump of gold in its inside, and in order to get the gold, they killed it. Having done so, they found to their surprise that the Hen differed in no respect from their other hens. The foolish pair, thus hoping to become rich all at once, deprived themselves of the gain of which they were assured day by day.

Quills #1: Expanding a Fable

The teacher will give you a simple fable. Your task will be to write an expanded fable by adding dialogue and colorful details. Remember to use colorful verbs.

Quills #2: Writing a Fable

The teacher will give you a list of "morals to the story." Your task will be to create a fable that teaches the moral.

DESCRIPTION

Chapter 2

Introduction

What is it to describe a person? Take Abraham Lincoln, for example. Probably no other public figure has been called "ugly" as many times as he was—mostly before and during his presidency. Yet, people who appreciate his great spirit have more often described his character. The difference can be seen in the paragraphs below. The first was written in 1862 by a London journalist describing Lincoln's physical appearance for his readers back in England:

> To say that he is ugly is nothing; to add that his figure is grotesque, is to convey no adequate impression. Fancy a man 6 feet high and thin out of proportion; with long bony arms and legs which somehow seem to be always in the way with great rugged furrowed hands which grab you like a vice when shaking yours; with a long scraggy neck and a chest too narrow for the great arms at his side. Add to this figure a head, coconut shaped and somewhat too small for such a stature, covered with rough uncombed and uncomable hair, that stands out in every direction at once. . . .[7]

Now look at a description of Lincoln's personality, written by Frederick Douglass, an escaped slave active in the abolitionist movement:

> I have been down there to see the President; and as you were not there, perhaps you would like to know how the President of the United States received a black man at the

White House. I will tell you how he received me—just as you see one gentleman receive another; with a hand and a voice, well balanced between a kind cordiality and a respectful reserve. I tell you I felt big there.[8]

From these two examples, you can get an idea of the many different approaches to description. You will have the chance to practice some of them in this chapter.

Methods of Describing People

In classical times, the composition teachers identified six methods that are used when describing people:

- Name
- Age
- Gender (male or female)
- Nationality (or ethnic group)
- Appearance
- Mental state
- Emotional state

> To help memorize these methods, you can turn them into an acronym by using the first letter of each word: **NAGNAME**.

EXERCISE 2.1: Examining a Classical Description

Directions: With your classmates, read this description about Julius Caesar, which is based on a description by the Roman writer Suetonius (AD 70-130). Then, as a class, look for the various methods Suetonius used in this description.

Julius Caesar (100 BC – 44 BC) was tall and light-skinned. His arms and legs were round, and he had a rather full face with black, piercing eyes. He had excellent health except that near the end of his life he had sudden fainting fits and did not sleep well. Twice in his life he was seized with the "falling sickness" (epilepsy) while in active service. He was extremely fussy in personal grooming. He kept the hair of his head closely cut and his face smoothly shaved. He was greatly bothered by his baldness, especially after he found himself the object of the jibes of his enemies. Therefore, he used to brush his hair forward from the crown of his head, and was greatly pleased that the Senate and People conferred honors on him that allowed him constantly to wear a laurel crown [see image]. It is said that he was particular in his dress, for he wore the *latus clavus* with fringes about the wrists.[9]

Name: What is the name of the person whom Suetonius is describing?

Age: Suetonius does not directly state an age, but he does describe an older man and talk about his health near the time of his death. Using the dates in the first sentence, figure out how old Caesar was at the time of his assassination in 44 BC.

Gender: Obviously Julius Caesar was a man, but what problem of older men seems to have afflicted Caesar?

Nationality: Though this paragraph does not directly state Caesar's nationality, indicate his nationality in the space provided.

Appearance:

    a. How did Caesar comb his hair?

    b. Was he tall or short?

    c. Was his skin dark or light toned?

    d. What did he often wear on his head?

    e. What decorative feature of clothing did he have around his wrists when he wore the *latus clavus* (a toga with a purple stripe)?

Mental/Emotional State: From the details about Caesar's hair and clothing, what can we assume about Caesar's personality?

EXERCISE 2.2: Examining a Description of a Person

Directions: Begin by reading this description of Huckleberry Finn, as narrated by his friend Tom Sawyer in the famous novel *The Adventures of Tom Sawyer* by Mark Twain (1835-1910). Then answer the questions that follow

Excerpt from *The Adventures of Tom Sawyer* By Mark Twain

(1) Shortly Tom came upon the juvenile pariah of the village, Huckleberry Finn, son of the town drunkard. (2) Huckleberry was cordially hated and dreaded by all the mothers of the town, because he was idle and lawless and vulgar and bad— and because all their children admired him so, and delighted in his forbidden society, and wished they dared to be like him. (3) Tom was like the rest of the respectable boys, in that he envied Huckleberry his gaudy outcast condition, and was under strict orders not to play with him. (4) So he played with him every time he got a chance. (5) Huckleberry was always dressed in the cast-off clothes of full-grown men, and they were in perennial bloom and fluttering with rags. (6) His hat was a vast ruin with a wide crescent lopped out of its brim; his coat, when he wore one, hung nearly to his heels and had the rearward buttons far down the back; but one suspender supported his trousers; the seat of the trousers bagged low and contained nothing, the fringed legs dragged in the dirt when not rolled up.

(7) Huckleberry came and went, at his own free will. (8) He slept on doorsteps in fine weather and in empty hogsheads in wet; he did not have to go to school or to church, or call any being master or obey anybody; he could go fishing or swimming when and where he chose, and stay as long as it suited him; nobody forbade him to fight; he could sit up as late as he pleased; he was always the first boy that went barefoot in the spring and the last to resume leather in the fall; he never had to wash, nor put on clean clothes; he could swear wonderfully. (9) In a word, everything that goes to make life precious that boy had. (10) So thought every harassed, hampered, respectable boy in St. Petersburg.[10]

Student Text

Questions

1. **Name:**

    Think briefly about the name Twain gave this character: Huckleberry Finn.

    - First of all, why do you think he gave him a name like "Huckleberry" instead of a traditional name such as Sam or Billy?

    - Secondly, according to the *Online Etymology Dictionary,* in the 1800's the word *huckleberry* sometimes referred to "a person of little consequence." Who in the town might have described Huck Finn that way?

2. **Age:**

    The author does not tell us directly how old Huckleberry Finn is, but he has planted some clues. Interpret the clues in these sentences:

    Sentence 1: What adjective describes *pariah*? What is the meaning of that adjective?

    Sentence 3: What noun does the adjective *respectable* modify?

    Sentence 4: What verb suggests the activities of a boy?

    Sentence 5: Here Twain describes Huckleberry by using contrast. He says that Huckleberry's clothing was the *opposite* of Huckleberry himself. For whom were the clothes made, and what does that tell us about Huck's age?

3. **Gender:**

   Sentence 8: Obviously, Huck Finn is a boy. What activities associated with boyhood are provided to emphasize why other boys envied him?

4. **Nationality or Ethnic Group:**

   Huckleberry Finn is an American boy in the southern United States in the nineteenth-century, but think a minute about his last name, Finn. Finn is an Irish surname, and in the time period when Twain was writing, the Irish were considered to be drunk, lazy, and unskilled. People did not want to hire them or live near them.

   Sentence 1: What characteristic often associated with the Irish is used to describe Huck's father? How does this add to Huckleberry's description?

5. **Appearance:**

   Sentences 5-6: In your own words, describe Huck's clothing.

6. **Mental and Emotional State:**

   Sentences 7-8: We are not told directly what Huckleberry Finn's mental state was, but based on Sentences 7-8, which of the following best describes what Twain was suggesting about Huck's mental and emotional state?

   A. He was sad.

   B. He liked school and learning.

   C. He was carefree.

   D. He was mean.

Tips for Writing Descriptions

Since classical times, good writers have employed certain methods to set their writing apart. In this chapter, we will look at two of them: specific details and figures of speech, and we will find examples in the writings of the classical author, Plutarch (AD 45-120).

Tip 1: Specific Details

When describing, use clear, specific details so that your readers can better picture what is being described. Avoid vague and unclear descriptions.

When writing about the exploits of Theseus, Plutarch reported that Theseus reached a place called Krommyon, which was famous for its wild beast. However, instead of simply saying, "Phaia was not an ordinary pig," Plutarch wrote, "Now the wild sow of Krommyon, whom they called Phaia, was no ordinary beast, but a fierce creature and hard to conquer" (Plutarch).[11]

Later, at the end of his narrative about Theseus, Plutarch described the search of the Athenians for Theseus' grave, which they eventually discovered by means of a miraculous sign. However, instead of simply saying, "They found a man's coffin with a weapon beside it," Plutarch wrote, "There was found the coffin of a man of great stature, and lying beside it a brazen lance-head and a sword".[12]

EXERCISE 2.3: Specific Details

Directions: Below are some sentences from *The Secret Garden* by Frances Hodgson Burnett (1849-1924). Burnett's sentences are quite specific. In the exercise, each sentence is incomplete. You will see two choices (A and B), which are both possible ways to finish the sentence. In the blank, place the letter of the phrase which you think was written by Frances Hodgson Burnett. That is to say, choose the more descriptive phrase.

_____ 1. The rain seemed to be streaming down more heavily than ever and everybody in the station. . . .
   A. was wearing a raincoat.
   B. wore wet and glistening waterproofs.

_____ 2. When she opened her eyes in the morning it was because a young housemaid had come into her room to light the fire and was kneeling on the hearth-rug. . . .
   A. raking out the cinders noisily.
   B. cleaning the fireplace.

_____ 3. When she stood still, she saw a bird with a bright red breast sitting on the topmost branch of one of them, and suddenly he burst into . . . —almost as if he had caught sight of her and was calling to her.
   A. a pretty song
   B. his winter song

_____ 4. He hopped about and pecked the earth briskly, looking for. . . .
   A. seeds and insects.
   B. something to eat.

_____ 5. She stopped with a little laugh of pleasure, and there, lo and behold, was the robin swaying on a. . . .
   A. long branch of ivy.
   B. a branch.

2. Figures of Speech

One way to describe something is to compare it to another thing. Our language is full of expressions such as "sharp as a tack" or "flatter than a pancake," which people use every day to communicate description. Though it is not a good idea to use expressions that are a bit worn out from over-use, it is always a good idea to create new and meaningful comparisons of your own. In fact, the ability to create fresh descriptions is one of the characteristics of a good writer.

Two figures of speech that make particularly descriptive comparisons are similes and metaphors.

- A *simile* is a comparison which uses *like* or *as*. Plutarch used a good simile in his "Life of Pericles," when he was describing a *samaina*. Instead of simply saying, "This is a ship that turns up in the front," Plutarch wrote, "This is a ship having a beak turned up *like* a swine's snout".[13]

- A *metaphor* is a comparison which does not use *like* or *as*. Instead, it often uses a form of *be* to equate two things. In Plutarch's "Life of Themistocles," we read about Timocreon, a Greek poet whom Themistocles had punished for sympathizing with the Persians. Timocreon later got a bit of revenge when Themistocles lost power and was exiled. Instead of simply stating, "I'm not the only one who lost his honor," Timocreon used a metaphor: "I'm not the only fox without a tail".[14] In this way, he compared himself to a wounded and embarrassed fox.

EXERCISE 2.4: Similes and Metaphors

Directions: Below are some lines of poetry by the Scottish author Robert Louis Stevenson (1850-1894).[15] If the lines contain a simile, put an *S* in the blank. If they contain a metaphor, put an *M* in the blank.

_____ 1. "My Bed Is a Boat" (title)

_____ 2. Grasses run like a green sea
O'er the lawn up to my knee.

_____ 3. I saw the dimpling river pass
And be the sky's blue looking-glass.

_____ 4. Black are my steps on silver sod;
Thick blows my frosty breath abroad;
And tree and house, and hill and lake,
Are frosted like a wedding-cake.

_____ 5. All of the sights of the hill and the plain
Fly as thick as driving rain.

Quills #1: Description of a Person

 Your teacher will give you the instructions you need to write a description of a person.

Topics for Describing Objects

When describing objects, focus on these topics:

a. Color

b. Size

c. Shape

d. Texture

e. Age

f. Material

g. Attribute

EXERCISE 2.5: Examining a Description of an Object

 Directions: Please begin by reading the description of Duncan Phyfe chairs. Then answer the questions that follow.

Duncan Phyfe Chair used with the kind permission of the Stanley Weiss Collection, Providence, RI

The Duncan Phyfe chair is a classic piece of American furniture. It was named for its designer, American cabinet maker Duncan Phyfe (1795-1848), a Scottish immigrant. The chair was made of mahogany, a reddish-brown hardwood which Phyfe imported in the early nineteenth-century from the West Indies. As shown in the picture, the bottom half of the front legs were carved, and the foot was in the shape of an animal's paw. The square-shaped seats were upholstered, often in a silky damask fabric. Duncan Phyfe tried to capture the designs of classical Greece in his furniture, as seen in this example where the back of the chair is in the shape of a lyre. Chairs of this style measured 32 ½ inches in height.

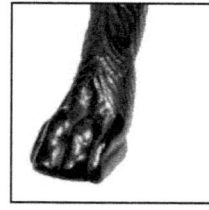

Detail of the foot. Note paw-like shape.

Topic	Detail
Color	Color of the mahogany:
Size	Height of the chair:
Shape	Shape of the front feet: Shape of the back: Shape of the seat:
Age	When manufactured?
Material	Seats:
Texture	Seats:
Attribute	Style Duncan Phyfe tried to capture:

EXERCISE 2.6: Examining a Description of an Object

Directions: Please read the description of an American football. Then complete the chart that follows.

A football is a ball made of leather (for professional and college play) or rubber (for youth and high school). The leather used to make footballs is tanned to a natural brown color. The ball is composed of four panels, which are stitched together except for one seam where white leather laces are used to finish the construction. The ball has what is called a "prolate spheroid" shape, meaning it is a

long sphere. This shape causes the ball to "spiral" and travel further. Except in the case of footballs used by professional teams, white stripes are painted on each end of the ball, halfway around the circumference of the ball. The color white makes it easier for players to see the ball during night games. The leather of a football has a pebbly texture. Together with the white leather laces, the texture makes it easier for players to grip the ball. Footballs are 11 inches long and 28 inches around. They weigh 14 to 15 ounces.

Topic	Detail
Color	Ball: Laces: Stripes:
Size	Inches long: Inches around: Weight:
Shape	
Texture	
Age	Not Applicable
Material	Professional and college: High school and youth leagues:
Attribute	Number of panels: Advantage of shape:

Quills #2: Description of an Object

 Your teacher will give you the instructions you need to write a description of an object.

NARRATIVE

Chapter 3

Introduction

Have you ever told ghost stories around a camp fire? Or, do you have a family member who can keep you interested for hours with war stories? What do you talk about with your friends while eating in the lunch room? Chances are you talk about what happened that morning or the previous night. It seems that almost everywhere a person goes, narrative is a big part of conversation.

The ancient Greeks understood this great human love for stories. Their word *mūthos*, which means *report* or *story*, is the source of our word *myth*. In English, this word refers to a special category of story, one which has perhaps superhuman elements. For a more straightforward report of the facts without such elements, speakers of English use the word *narrative*, which comes from the Latin word *narrāre*, *to tell* or *to narrate*.

Because stories form the lion's share of what we talk about with each other, the teachers in ancient Greece greatly emphasized them. Fables, myths, and narratives are among the first exercises of the progymnasmata, but the use of narrative is not left by the wayside as students move farther into the progymnasmata. Rather, narrative plays a key role in almost every one of the exercises. In short, narrative is the foundation of classical composition.

Definition and Purpose of the Narrative

1. Narrative is defined as a story that tells about something that happened in the past.

2. Narratives have many purposes.

   a. In the form of fiction, writers use them as a form of entertainment.
   b. In the newspaper, journalists use them to communicate current events to the general public.
   c. In a courtroom, lawyers use them to explain a crime to a jury.
   d. In the classroom, teachers use them to explain human history.
   e. At church, pastors use them to help the congregation understand God's plan.

 **THINK IT THROUGH:** Why do you think people enjoy stories so much? Why do you think we *need* stories so much?

 **THINK IT THROUGH:** What two narratives did Moses use to begin the book of Genesis? Why do you think that beginning with those narratives was better than starting with, say, definitions of *sin* and *salvation*?

Types of Narratives

One can find many types of narratives, but here we will discuss two: the mythical narrative and the historical narrative.

Type One: The Mythical Narrative

Characteristics

1. In ancient Greece and Rome, the mythical narrative was a tale or a legend about gods or heroes.

2. Like the fable, the mythical narrative can be used to teach a moral.

3. A mythical narrative differs from a fable in three ways:

   a. The characters are heroic humans, not animals or objects. In classical times, the characters sometimes included gods or goddesses as well.

   b. The characters normally have names.

   c. The stories often involve superhuman accomplishments.

   d. The moral to the story is *not* normally expressed at the end of the tale.

Model Mythical Narrative

Theseus and the Minotaur

A horrible monster called a Minotaur lived in a maze at the palace of King Minos in Crete. The maze was extremely complicated. No one who entered could ever find the way out alive, so Minos found it convenient to imprison his enemies there so that the monster could feed on them. One day King Minos' son traveled to Athens to participate in the annual athletic contests, but during the Marathon he was killed by Athenians who were jealous of his success in the games. Minos was so furious at his son's murder that he made a terrible demand of the king of Athens. He ordered him to send seven young men and seven young women to Crete every year so that he could feed them to the Minotaur.

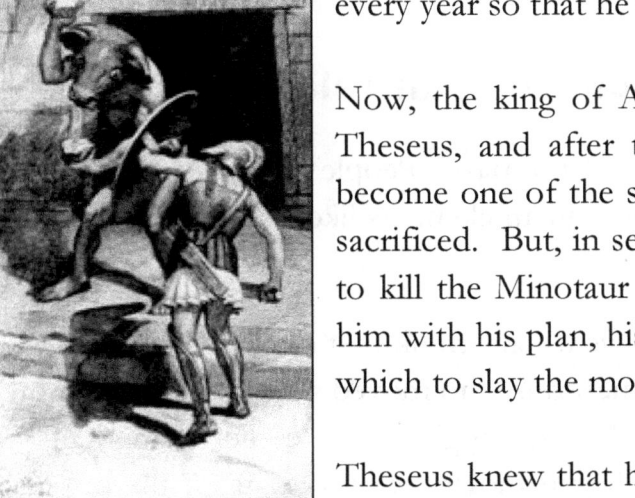

Now, the king of Athens also had a son. His name was Theseus, and after three years, he decided that he should become one of the seven lads who would go to Crete to be sacrificed. But, in secret, he told his father that his goal was to kill the Minotaur and end the human sacrifices. To help him with his plan, his father gave him a powerful sword with which to slay the monster.

Theseus knew that he would be able to enter the maze, but how to escape after killing the Minotaur was another matter.

To find a solution, he befriended King Minos' daughter, and she decided to help him. She gave him a ball of thread and told him to tie it to the gate at the entrance of the maze, then gradually release the thread behind him as he advanced forward into the maze. Then, when the time was right, he could follow it back out. Theseus took her advice. Upon reaching the Minotaur, he swung his father's sword three times, slashing the Minotaur's throat and causing him to fall to earth dead. Happily, he then sheathed his sword, led the other young men and women out of the maze, and sailed back home to Athens with all of them, ending Athens' debt to King Minos.

EXERCISE 3.1: Examining a Mythical Narrative

Directions: Answer the following questions about the legend "Theseus and the Minotaur."

1. Does the story concern humans, gods, beasts, or a mixture?

2. What traits does Theseus possess that make us admire him?

3. What do you consider to be the moral to this story?

Mythical Narratives in America: The Tall Tale

The mythical narrative is not just a relic of the past. People still enjoy spinning yarns and telling *tall tales*, stories which include superhuman elements like lassoing the moon or leaping the Grand Canyon.

When we think of the American tall tale, we usually think first of characters Paul Bunyan and Pecos Bill, who represent the spirit of Americans who moved west to build a nation after the Civil War. But the American tall tale had its origins even earlier than that. After the Revolutionary War, the new Americans began moving westward from the original thirteen colonies. This westward expansion, like the one that would follow after the Civil War, brought European-Americans into wilderness areas which had many challenges from the climate, the land, and the wildlife.

One man has come to represent the settlers who moved "up West" at this time—Davy Crockett (1786-1836). Davy made the history books by being the first man elected to represent the new state of Tennessee in the United States House of Representatives and for volunteering to defend the Alamo, where he died in the Battle of the Alamo in 1836. But what we want to examine here is the Davy Crockett who became legendary in the early 1800s in a publication called the *Davy Crockett Almanack*.

Though educated men founded and governed the country, it was the man of action who came to the fore in Davy's day. In the tales about Davy and his larger-than-life family, we see the many threats to life on the frontier in Davy's Tennessee home. Alligators, bears, snakes, catamounts (panthers), wolves, and eagles all figure largely in Davy's tales, not to mention the rascally raccoon which Davy turned into his signature head wear (at least as the legend would have it).

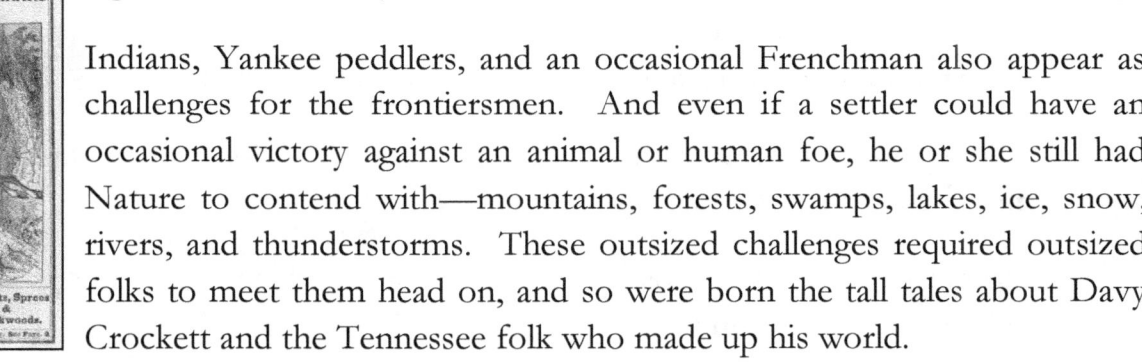

Indians, Yankee peddlers, and an occasional Frenchman also appear as challenges for the frontiersmen. And even if a settler could have an occasional victory against an animal or human foe, he or she still had Nature to contend with—mountains, forests, swamps, lakes, ice, snow, rivers, and thunderstorms. These outsized challenges required outsized folks to meet them head on, and so were born the tall tales about Davy Crockett and the Tennessee folk who made up his world.

Model Tall Tale

Teazer
By Davy Crockett

The best dog that ever I owned, war named Teazer. Besides that, I had Tearer, Holdfast, Deathmaul, Grim, Porcupine and Growler, that I've got now. Teazer was the best of the hull lot, and he died one day, bekase when I ordered him to dive in the Mississippi, I forgot to give him the word to come up to the top o' the water, and he wouldn't presume to put his nose above water without orders. He war the only dog I ever owned that war true grit; an the way he could throw a buffalo war astonishment to all my other dogs. He war in his eightieth year when he died.[16]

Characteristics of the American Tall Tale

The American tall tale has several key characteristics.

1. **Setting:** The tall tale usually has a wilderness setting.

    a. Davy Crockett's tall tales were set in the mountains of his home state of Tennessee.

    b. The Paul Bunyan stories were set in the logging regions of Wisconsin.

    c. The Pecos Bill stories were set on the Plains or in the desert of the southwest.

2. **Characters:** The main characters are often larger-than-life men and women of superhuman strength who can easily handle the gigantic problems that faced the settlers.

3. **Techniques:**

    a. One technique of the tall tale is *hyperbole* (hī PER bə lē), which is the use of exaggeration to make a special effect. Here is one example:

    "About Paul Bunyan's gigantic blue ox, it was said, "Some of the lakes in Minnesota and Wisconsin are in holes made by his feet."[17]

    b. Another technique is the use of *simile* (SĬM ə lē), which is a comparison using *like* or *as*. Here are some examples:

    "Every winter she fatted up on bear's meat, so that when she turned out in spring, she war bigger round than a whiskey barrel; and when I put my arms 'round the creatur, it war *like* hugging a bale of cotton."

    "Seven men were kept busy with wheelbarrows hauling prune stones away from the camp. The chipmunks ate these and grew *as* big *as* tigers."

4. **Language:** The narrator uses "folksy" language. This technique tries to catch the dialect of the people who created the tale.

    a. It includes spellings that represent the pronunciation of the people. For example, the word *for* might be spelled as *fer*. The word *against* might be spelled as *agin*. Here is an example from the Davy Crockett tales:

"This gal was named Jerusa Stubbs, and had only one eye, but that was *pritty* enough for two."[18]

b. The language might include non-standard English, what some people might call "bad grammar." That is because the stories originated with the practical people building the country, not the "city folk" of the East. Here is an example:

"Then I *seed* I *couldn't do nothing* with my arms, for they war fastened by the snakes like ropes."

c. Tall tale narrators might even make up a few words of their own, as in this line:

"We had some of the most *ragiferous* fights with Alligators."

EXERCISE 3.2: Examining a Tall Tale

Directions: Below is a tall tale which centers around Davy Crockett's younger daughter. Please read the tale and answer the questions that follow.

Crockett, Fishing in the Atlantic

Taken a notion to have some salt fish naturally pickled, an caught all on my own hook, I jist tied up line enough to reach to the bottom o' the sea, which you know haint any bottom at all. I took a walk down to the old Atlantic, baited my alligator hook with a piece o' the hind quarter of fresh pork, walked out to the limb of an uprooted tree, and set in for a day's sport o' salt water fishen. Well, I throwed out about two mile o' my line with a hull rock for a dipsy; it war about two hours in runnen to the eend on't. Well, arter it had been down about two seconds an a quarter, I suddenaciously felt a bite nearly as strong as a fifteen year old alligator, and a tarna heavy pull down the stream. I rolled about a mile o' my line upon my fishin pole; then calculatin that I had a tall prize tight and safe, I gin a twenty-horse-power jerk and swing; a tarnal big splash follered; an dreckly I felt something grabbin me by the neck about as tight as a hungry barr, and biten a piece o' Crockett meat out o' my left shoulder; so I says, "Mr. Sea Fish, although I gin you a bite, I don't stand your biten me." I grabbed the thing about the neck, pulled it right down before me, held it between my two paws, an took a savage grin at it, an by all the walkin creation, it war the strangest critter I ever did see; it war half dog, half frog, and t'other half human natur. No seamen, even Ben

Hardin, had ever seen such an eternal queer fish, an if any body will fetch me a feller to it, salt me if I don't fight with him which shall take both, for it are the queerest critter that ever old natur poked life into.[19]

Questions:

1. Underline one example of hyperbole.

2. Write down at least one example of superhuman strength from this tale.

3. Write down an example where the spelling shows the way a word was pronounced in Davy's dialect.

4. Copy one example of non-standard English grammar.

5. Give one example of a word that seems to have been made up.

Quills #1: Writing a Tall Tale

 Your teacher will provide you with a composition assignment so that you can show your ability to write a Tall Tale.

Type Two: The Historical Narrative

The Historical Narrative has three main characteristics:

1. The historical narrative tells about an important event in the past.

2. It is often used at times of celebration, such as the narrative of the Pilgrims, which is recounted at Thanksgiving.

3. Like the fable and the mythical narrative, the historical narrative can teach a lesson about life.

THINK IT THROUGH: What patriotic narratives are associated with Independence Day (the Fourth of July)? What Bible narratives are associated with Christian holidays?

Model Historical Narrative

Excerpt from "Daniel Boone: The Boy of the Frontier (1735-1820)" By Rupert S. Holland

[1] But life was not all sport for the young Boones. Various Indian tribes, the Catawbas, the Cherokees, and the Shawnese [*sic*] hunted not far away, and although they were often on friendly terms with the whites, and came to the settlement to trade, sometimes they put on their war paint, and descended on the small frontier homes with full fury.

The Shooting of General Braddock at Fort Duquesne, 1755
By Edwin Willard Deming

[2] As the French came down from the north, disputing this new land with the English settlers, they made the Indians their allies, and the border warfare grew more bitter. Finally, the English general [Edward] Braddock decided to march west himself and try to teach the French and Indians a lesson.

[3] It was not likely that such a sturdy youth as Daniel Boone could resist the desire to march against the French. The expedition [of 1755] promised him a chance to push farther into that wild western country, if nothing else, and so he joined Braddock's small army with about a hundred other North Carolina frontiersmen. Daniel was made chief wagoner and blacksmith.

[4] General Braddock knew nothing of Indian warfare, and the little expedition proved an easy target for their enemies. The cumbersome and heavily laden baggage wagons were a great handicap to them. The English regulars, the frontiersmen, and the baggage train were caught in the deep ravine of Turtle Creek [a tributary of the Monongahela River], a few miles away from Pittsburg, and suddenly set upon by ambushed Indians commanded by French officers. Many of the drivers, caught in the trap, were killed. Daniel, however, contrived to cut the traces of his team, and mounting one of the horses, escaped down and out of the ravine under a fire of shot and arrows.

[5] The Indians pursued the fugitives, laying waste the borders of Pennsylvania and Virginia, but not following as far south as the Yadkin. Daniel reached home, and set to work to strengthen the settlement's ties of friendship with the two tribes of the neighborhood, the Catawbas and the Cherokees. With their aid he was able to provide sufficient safeguard against the Northern tribes.[20]

EXERCISE 3.3: Historical Narrative

Directions: Please answer the questions below about "Daniel Boone, The Boy of the Frontier (1735-1820)."

1. The reading about Daniel Boone printed here is an excerpt from a longer chapter. By looking at the first sentence of the excerpt, can you guess what the subject of the previous paragraphs was? Write what you think it was in the space provided.

2. This excerpt tells about Daniel Boone's participation in the French and Indian Wars, which lasted off and on from 1689 to 1763. These questions about Paragraph 2 help you examine the writer's technique of communicating basic elements to the reader.

   a. What two European powers were fighting each other?

   b. According to the information in Paragraph 2, with whom were the Indians allied?

3. Now skip forward to Paragraph 5. With whom did Daniel Boone help to forge an Indian alliance for the English?

4. Historical narrative often tries to explain *why* things happened the way they did. In the next few questions, focus on cause and effect.

   a. Paragraph 3: Why was Boone attracted to the French and Indian War?

   b. Paragraph 4: Why was the English general Braddock having so much trouble?

   c. Paragraph 4: Why did the English become so bogged down in the ravine?

5. Historical narratives often concern challenges, wars, and failures, but in the English-speaking tradition, writers like to end on a positive note, perhaps pointing to a better future. Does the author Rupert S. Holland do so in this excerpt? Explain your answer.

The Daniel Boone half-dollar was issued from 1934 to 1938 in honor of the bicentennial birth date of Daniel Boone.

Six Elements of the Narrative

Teachers in classical times identified the six elements of a narrative in this way:

Agent
Action
Time
Place
Cause
Manner

Fortunately, speakers of English have found an easier way to remember these elements, listing them as question words, thus:

Who?
What?
When?
Where?
Why?
How?

THINK IT THROUGH: As a class, return to the story "Daniel Boone, The Boy of the Frontier (1735-1820)." On the board, specify each of the elements:

a. Who was the main character in the narrative?

b. What did the main character do?

c. When did the action take place?

d. Where did the action take place?

e. Why was Braddock defeated?

f. How did Daniel Boone escape?

Retelling a Narrative

Sometimes in life we need the skill of retelling a narrative. In classical times, teachers taught several ways to do that. Here we will look at two of them.

Shortening a Narrative

Often in school, history teachers ask students to write summaries of what they have read. The best summaries of narratives are those that focus on the six basic elements listed above: *who, what, when, where, why,* and *how*. In a summary, the writer uses his or her own words to report these elements. This technique is called paraphrase. The models and exercises below focus on that skill.

Model Shortened Narrative

The Cumberland Gap
(Original Narrative)

The Cumberland Gap is a pass through the Cumberland Mountains at the point where the corners of Kentucky, Virginia, and Tennessee come together. It had long been used by the Indians, and when it was discovered by Dr. Thomas Walker, a doctor and explorer from Virginia, in 1750, he knew it could be a great help to the settlers as well. The Cumberland Gap played an important role in colonial history. Daniel Boone and a team of frontiersmen blazed the Wilderness Road through the Gap in 1775, making it easier for pioneers to bring wagons and livestock into the region for settlement. As a result of the Cumberland Gap, the western boundary of the original thirteen colonies came to extend all the way to the Mississippi River.

(113 words)

Boone at Cumberland Gap
Courtesy of U.S. Capitol
Historical Society

The Cumberland Gap
(Shortened Narrative)

The Cumberland Gap is a pass through the Cumberland Mountains. Dr. Thomas Walker discovered it in 1750, and Daniel Boone blazed the Wilderness Road through the Gap in 1775, opening the area for settlement. The Gap allowed westward expansion to the Mississippi River.

(46 words)

Paraphrasing

When teachers make assignments, they often say, "Please write your report in your own words." Writing something in your own words is very important for two reasons:

a. It helps the teacher to see that the student has indeed understood the reading.

b. It helps the student steer clear of the charge of cheating. In the United States, copying someone else's words is considered the same as "stealing" from the author. However, summarizing a piece of writing in one's own words is considered fair to both the author and the paraphraser.

Example:

Original: "Although the Cherokees were often on friendly terms with the whites, and came to the settlement to trade, sometimes they put on their war paint, and descended on the small frontier homes with full fury."

Paraphrase: The Cherokees were often friendly to the whites and traded with them, but sometimes they attacked the settlers' homes.

Techniques of Paraphrasing

Below are two specific changes you can make to put a sentence into your own words.

1. Use a synonym, usually an easier word.

    "The Gap was a good hunting *territory*."

    ➢ The Gap was a good hunting *area*."

2. Change a noun to a verb, or *vice versa*.

    "By 1796 the Wilderness Road had given passage to as many as 200,000 *travelers*."

    ➢ By 1796, 200,000 people *had traveled* the Wilderness Road."

3. Omit information that is not necessary.

    "Tourists can visit the Hensley Settlement, *an early 20th-century Kentucky mountain community that has been preserved by the National Park Service as representative of* the early settler's life *on top of Brush Mountain*"

    ➢ "Tourists can visit the Hensley Settlement, which shows the early settlers' way of life."

EXERCISE 3.4: Paraphrase Practice

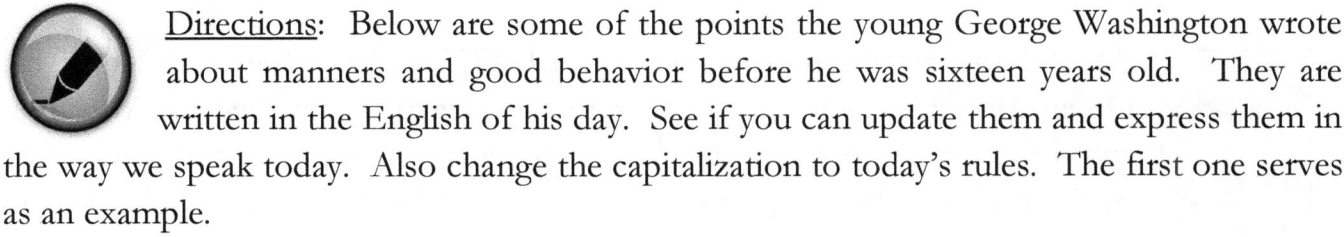

Directions: Below are some of the points the young George Washington wrote about manners and good behavior before he was sixteen years old. They are written in the English of his day. See if you can update them and express them in the way we speak today. Also change the capitalization to today's rules. The first one serves as an example.

1. **Then:** "Every Action done in Company, ought to be with Some Sign of Respect, to those that are Present."

    Now:

2. **Then:** "If You Cough, Sneeze, Sigh, or Yawn, do it not Loud but Privately."

   Now:

3. **Then:** "Turn not your Back to others especially in Speaking, Jog not the Table or Desk on which Another reads or writes, lean not upon any one."

   Now:

4. **Then:** "Be no Flatterer, neither Play with any that delights not to be Play'd Withal."

   Now:

5. **Then:** "Reproach none for the Infirmities of Nature, nor Delight to Put them that have [them] in mind thereof."

   Now:

EXERCISE 3.5: Retelling a Narrative

Directions: Below is a short historical narrative about the capture of Fort Ticonderoga in May 1775. After reading it, identify the six basic elements of the narrative by filling out the chart. Then retell the narrative in your own words.

Ethan Allen Captures Fort Ticonderoga

At 2:00 a.m. on the morning of May 10, 1775, Ethan Allan and 230 of his Green Mountain Boys, a militia from the area that later became Vermont, stood poised to cross Lake Champlain to Fort Ticonderoga, which was held by the British. Their hope was to wrest the fort from the British soldiers who had attacked the Americans at Lexington and Concord in April. It took longer than they had hoped to round up enough boats to carry them across, and only eighty-three had made it by the time they realized that the sun would rise before they could get all of the men to the

east side of the lake. The element of surprise was key, so the eighty-three men pushed on alone. When they reached the fort near dawn, they easily subdued a sentry and demanded that he lead them to the British commander, Captain William Delaplace, who came to the door in his night clothes. When Delaplace questioned them in whose name they came, Allan replied, "In the name of the Great Jehovah and the Continental Congress!" Delaplace surrendered the fort without incident. Fort Ticonderoga was now in the hands of the Americans.

Identify the basic elements of the narrative in the chart below. Then on another piece of paper, retell the narrative of the capture of Fort Ticonderoga in your own words, writing directly from the details on the chart without looking at the original.

Element	Details
Who?	Participants:
What?	What the Americans accomplished:
When?	Date: Time of day:
Where?	Location of fort:
Why?	Reason for taking the fort:
How?	How the hour helped them: How they gained access to the commander:

Quills #2: Writing a Historical Narrative

 Your teacher will provide you with a composition assignment so that you can show your ability to write a Historical Narrative.

WRITING A GOOD PARAGRAPH

Chapter 4

Introduction

When we start to consider how we should organize our thoughts in a composition, we should look for the best advice. Thankfully, during his ministry, Jesus addressed this issue when he spoke to his disciples in the Sermon on the Mount about how they should pray. We find his words in Matthew 6:7-13, presented here in the King James Version of the Bible:

> [7] But when ye pray, use not vain repetitions, as the heathen do: for they think that they shall be heard for their much speaking.
>
> [8] Be not ye therefore like unto them: for your Father knoweth what things ye have need of, before ye ask him.
>
> [9] After this manner therefore pray ye: Our Father which art in heaven, Hallowed be thy name.
>
> [10] Thy kingdom come, Thy will be done in earth, as it is in heaven.
>
> [11] Give us this day our daily bread.
>
> [12] And forgive us our debts, as we forgive our debtors.
>
> [13] And lead us not into temptation, but deliver us from evil: For thine is the kingdom, and the power, and the glory, forever. Amen.

This, of course, you will recognize as the Lord's Prayer, and over the centuries this particular translation of Jesus' words has influenced communication in the English-speaking world.

What can we learn from this teaching, as far as it concerns us here in a composition textbook?

Notice that in Verse 7, the Lord says we should not use "vain repetitions" when we pray. Let's begin with the noun *repetitions*. Here we are being told that we should not just repeat the same thing over and over. Rather, we should be direct—say it once and move on. The noun *repetitions* is modified by the adjective *vain*, which means about the same thing as *meaningless*. So the Lord has told us that, when we communicate, we should NOT just repeat meaningless words and phrases over and over again. When talking to the Lord, *much speaking*—or meaningless repetitions—is not what counts. The model provided in the Lord's Prayer contains only five sentences, and yet is sufficient, as the Lord says, for our prayers.

The English-speaking world has come to use this direct, meaningful, and brief style of speaking in all of its communication, as you will see in the pages of this chapter.

Purpose and Definitions

1. The organization pattern introduced in this chapter is used to communicate factual information to people. It is not a pattern for a narrative, which you practiced in the first three chapters of this book. Instead, it goes by the name *expository writing*. The word *expository* comes from the Latin word *exponere*, which means *to explain, to set forth*. Therefore, paragraphs that explain something or set forth new information are called *expository paragraphs*.

2. A *paragraph* can be defined as a group of sentences that explain one idea.

3. The main idea of the paragraph is set forth in one general statement, called the *topic sentence*. The topic sentence is usually the first sentence of the paragraph. The remaining sentences of the paragraph then go on to explain the main idea.

4. Just as no one wants to get lost in the woods, so no one wants to get lost in someone else's words! Therefore, as we write paragraphs in

English, we use certain words to help guide readers through the information. Some examples are words like *first, second,* and *last.* These words are called *transitions.*

5. The word *transition* comes from the Latin word *transīre,* which means *to go across.* So just as travelers might go across a desert, readers "go across" or "transit" a paragraph. As road signs help travelers, so transition words help readers navigate their way through a paragraph.

Model Paragraph

Let's begin by looking at a finished paragraph and then examining the process used to create it. Imagine a situation where a social studies teacher asked the students to write about the history of a sport. One student, whom we will call Kip, decided to write about sports that were invented on the American continent. He then did some reading in the library or online about the history of the sport. Below is a copy of the paragraph he ultimately wrote and turned in to the teacher:

Sports Invented in America

(1) Three sports were invented on the American continent. (2) The first is lacrosse, which was created by Native Americans of the Iroquois tribe. (3) It was well-established by the 1600s when Jesuit missionaries in Canada wrote about it. (4) The second is basketball, which was created by Jim Naismith, a leader at the YMCA in Springfield, Massachusetts. (5) In 1891, he invented the game for lads to play indoors when it was too cold to go outdoors. (6) The third is American football. (7) Based on English rugby, American football was greatly influenced by Walter Chauncey Camp, who played football at Yale from 1888 to 1892 and helped develop the rules of football until his death in 1925. (8) In conclusion, three team sports were created and developed right here in America: lacrosse, basketball, and football.

In this paragraph, Kip has used the standard direct method of English paragraph writing. In the next few sections, we will examine the methods Kip used to compose this paragraph and then do some practice.

Topic Sentence

When writing a paragraph in English, the first thing writers must do is identify the topic and the specific thing they want to say about the topic. These two components are called the *general topic (GT)* and the *controlling idea (CI)*, and together they make up the *topic sentence (TS)*.

Topic Sentence = General Topic + Controlling Idea

Kip's topic and controlling idea break down this way:

General Topic = Sports

Controlling Idea = Invented on the American continent

Using these two parts, he wrote his topic sentence:

Topic Sentence = There are three sports which were invented on the American continent.

In conclusion, a topic sentence consists of two main parts: the general topic and the controlling idea.

EXERCISE 4.1: Identifying General Topic and Controlling Idea

Directions: In the topic sentences below, place the letters *GT* below the general topic and the letters *CI* below the controlling idea. The first one serves as an example.

1. Three <u>dog breeds</u> make especially <u>good pets</u>.
          GT   CI

2. Some video games can actually develop your brain.

3. Several places in my city make good tourist sites.

4. Baseball cards can be displayed in three main ways.

5. Mark Twain is famous for two novels about boyhood in the 1800s.

6. Our class members enjoy several activities at recess.

Writing a Conclusion

At the end of a paragraph, writers frequently add a one-sentence conclusion. One way to think of a conclusion is to view it as an echo of the topic sentence. That is, like the topic sentence, the conclusion re-states the main idea and the controlling idea. Its purpose is to sum up everything at the end of the paragraph.

In Kip's paragraph about sports invented in America, notice how the topic sentence (#1) and the conclusion (#8) have three similarities and three differences.

Sports Invented in America

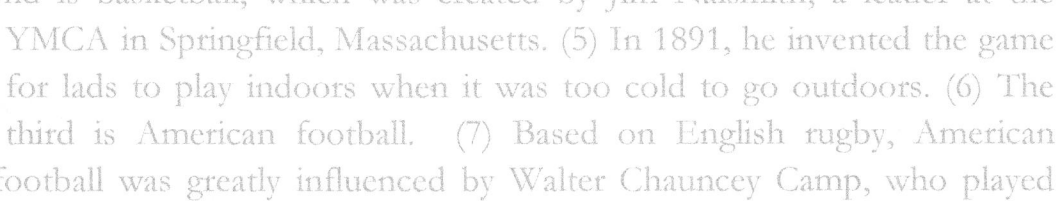

(1) Three sports were invented on the American continent. (2) The first is lacrosse, which was created by Native Americans of the Iroquois tribe. (3) It was well-established by the 1600s when Jesuit missionaries in Canada wrote about it. (4) The second is basketball, which was created by Jim Naismith, a leader at the YMCA in Springfield, Massachusetts. (5) In 1891, he invented the game for lads to play indoors when it was too cold to go outdoors. (6) The third is American football. (7) Based on English rugby, American football was greatly influenced by Walter Chauncey Camp, who played football at Yale from 1888 to 1892 and helped develop the rules of football until his death in 1925. **(8) In conclusion, three team sports were created and developed right here in America: lacrosse, basketball, and football.**

<u>Similarities</u>:
a. Both are general (that is, they have no details).
b. Both state the general topic.
c. Both state the controlling idea.

Differences:

a. The conclusion begins with a transition.
b. The sentences use slightly different wording.
c. *Optional:* The three specific points (the three sports) are named.

THINK IT THROUGH: What is the transition in Sentence #8? Why do you think it is a good idea to use such a transition?

THINK IT THROUGH: In the blank for each Sentence #8, write the re-wording of the phrase from Sentence #1 above it

a. Sentence #1: *three sports* _____

   Sentence #8: _____

b. Sentence #1: *were invented* _____

   Sentence #8: _____

c. Sentence #1: *on the American continent* _____

   Sentence #8: _____

NOTE: When making a zigzag scheme for a paragraph that contains a conclusion, the number of the concluding sentence (in this case #8) must appear in line with the number of the topic sentence (#1). That is because they are both general. (Note the position of the number *8* directly below the number *1*.)

Similarly, numbers *2, 4,* and *6* line up because they mark the main points, and numbers *3, 5,* and *7* line up because they mark the details.

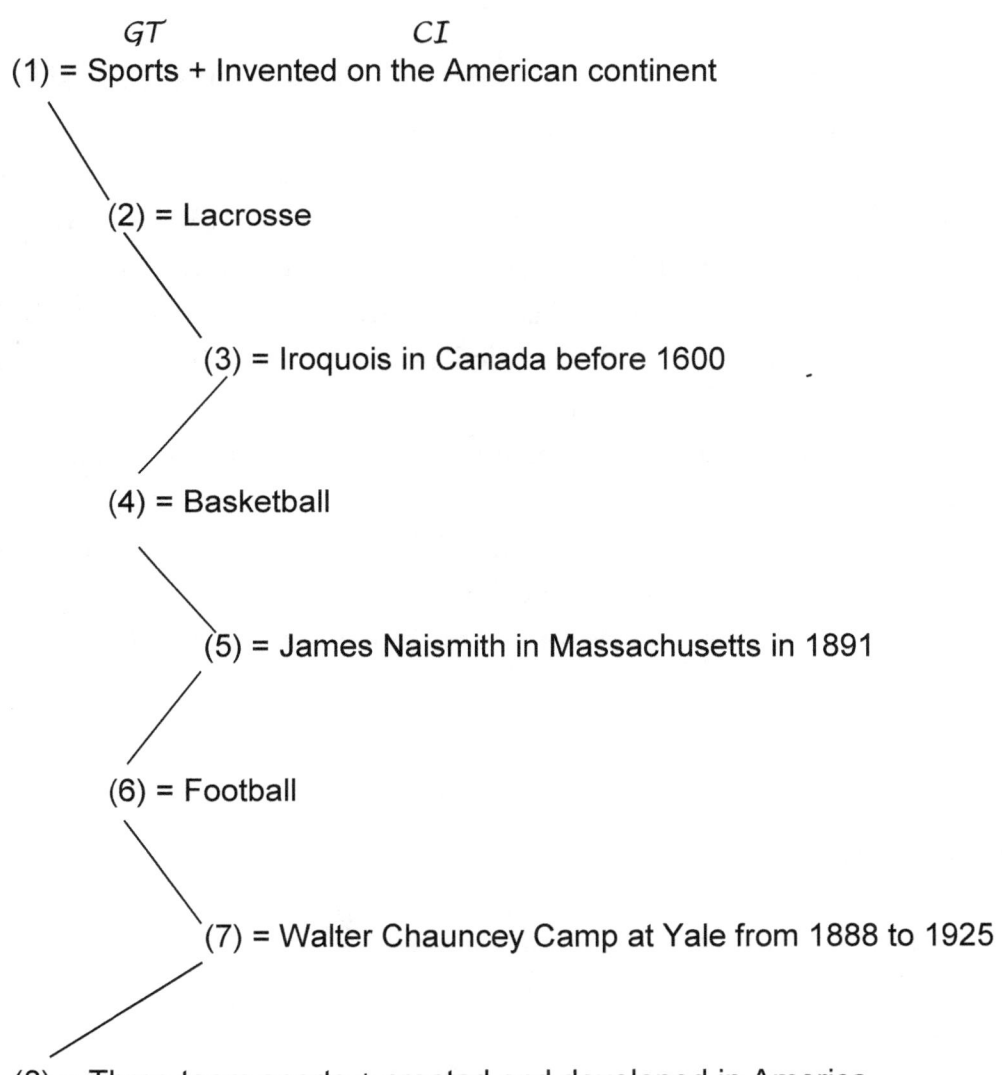

EXERCISE 4.2: Placing the Conclusion in a Zigzag Scheme

Directions: Below is a paragraph that contains a topic sentence, three points with a detail for each, and a conclusion. On another piece of paper, prepare a zigzag scheme that shows that the topic sentence and the conclusion are both general.

The Three Ships of Columbus

(1) Sailors on Christopher Columbus's three ships—the *Niña*, the *Pinta*, and the *Santa Maria*—left each ship a memorable story. (2) First, on the voyage west, the sailors on the *Niña* slept on deck. (3) However, on the return voyage, they adopted the use of the hammock, which they had seen among the natives in the West Indies. (4) Second, the story of the *Pinta* is tied up with that of its colorful captain, Martín Alonzo Pinzón. (5) On November 21, 1492, near Cuba, Pinzón disobeyed Columbus's command and sailed off from the other two ships for several weeks—probably in search of gold. (6) Last, there is the story of the wrecking of the *Santa Maria*, which happened late on December 24, 1492. (7) When the steersman went to sleep, leaving the helm in the hands of a cabin boy, the ship ran aground and was wrecked. (8) In short, mariners on the ships that sailed with Columbus provided us with interesting stories.

Paragraphs that List

There is one more thing to say about information paragraphs: they often are organized as lists. For that reason, the topic sentence often uses a word that suggests a list is coming. Notice, for example, the highlighted word in Kip's topic sentence:

> There are three sports which were invented on the American continent.

This word is called a *listing signal*. It could be a specific number such as *two* or *three*, or it could be an indefinite word such as *several* or *many*. Its purpose is to tip off the reader that a list is to follow. Here are some examples of topic sentences for the list type of paragraph:

   a. There are three changes I would like to make to my room.

b. Robert Louis Stevenson is a popular author for several reasons.

c. Trees can be divided into two main types.

EXERCISE 4.3: Finding Listing Signals

Directions: The sentences from Exercise 4.1 are reprinted below. This time, underline the listing signal in each one. Again, the first one serves as an example.

1. <u>Three</u> dog breeds make especially good pets.

2. Some video games can actually develop your brain.

3. Several places in my city make good tourist sites.

4. Baseball cards can be displayed in three main ways.

5. Mark Twain is famous for two novels about boyhood in the 1800s.

6. Our class members enjoy several activities at recess.

Zigzag Organization (from General to Specific)

Have you ever played the game called Categories? In this game, players slap their laps and clap their hands to create a rhythm. The leader throws out a general category. Then every time the fingers are snapped, a player takes a turn to name a specific member of that category. Here is an example:

Slap *Slap* / *Clap* *Clap*

    Snap *Snap* GROUP: Categories!

Slap *Slap* / *Clap* *Clap*

    Snap *Snap* GROUP: Such as!

Slap *Slap* / *Clap* *Clap*

Snap *Snap* **LEADER:** Classroom items!

Slap *Slap* / *Clap* *Clap*

Snap *Snap* **PLAYER A:** Globes!

Slap *Slap* / *Clap* *Clap*

Snap *Snap* **PLAYER B:** Dictionaries!

Slap *Slap* / *Clap* *Clap*

Snap *Snap* **PLAYER C:** Desks!

Slap *Slap* / *Clap* *Clap*

Snap *Snap* **PLAYER D:** White board!

The game continues in this way until a player cannot think of another specific member of the category.

The Categories game illustrates how a paragraph is organized in English. In short, we start with the more general statement (*classroom items*) and then move to the more specific topic (*globes*).

This pattern can be seen in Kip's first two sentences:

> (1) Three sports were invented on the American continent. (2) The first is lacrosse, which was created by Native Americans of the Iroquois tribe.

Notice that Kip has moved from general to specific. Sentence 1 is the more general statement because it refers to "three sports," in general. It does not name any particular sports.

Sentence 2, however, is more specific because it specifically names lacrosse. Thus, Kip has correctly moved from general (Sentence 1) to specific (Sentence 2).

Now, it is not enough for Kip just to tell the name of the sports. Since he is writing a history about sports invented on the American continent, he must now tell exactly *where* and *when* each sport was invented. Therefore, Kip uses Sentence 3 to add the *more* specific details:

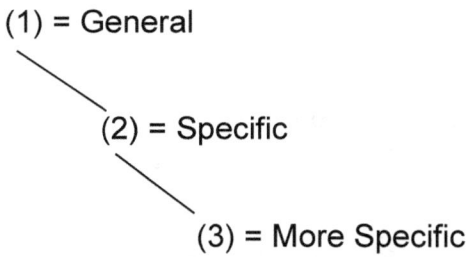(1) Three sports were invented on the American continent. (2) The first is lacrosse, which was created by Native Americans of the Iroquois tribe. (3) It was well-established by the 1600's when Jesuit missionaries in Canada wrote about it.

A scheme of the listing method looks like this:

(1) = General

    (2) = Specific

        (3) = More Specific

If we insert the information from Kip's paper, the scheme looks like this:

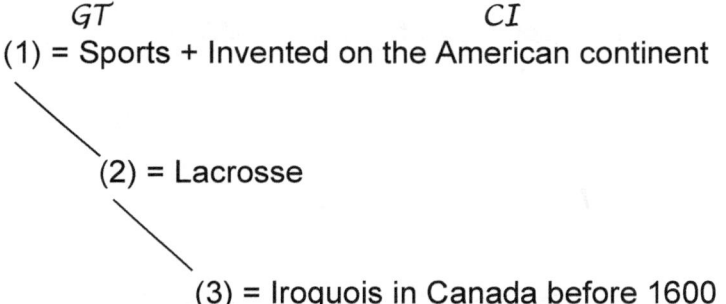

But lacrosse was just Kip's first point. Having given that point and its detail, he needed to move to his second point, basketball, and the detail about that sport. Then he added his third point and its detail. When finished, the complete scheme looked like this:

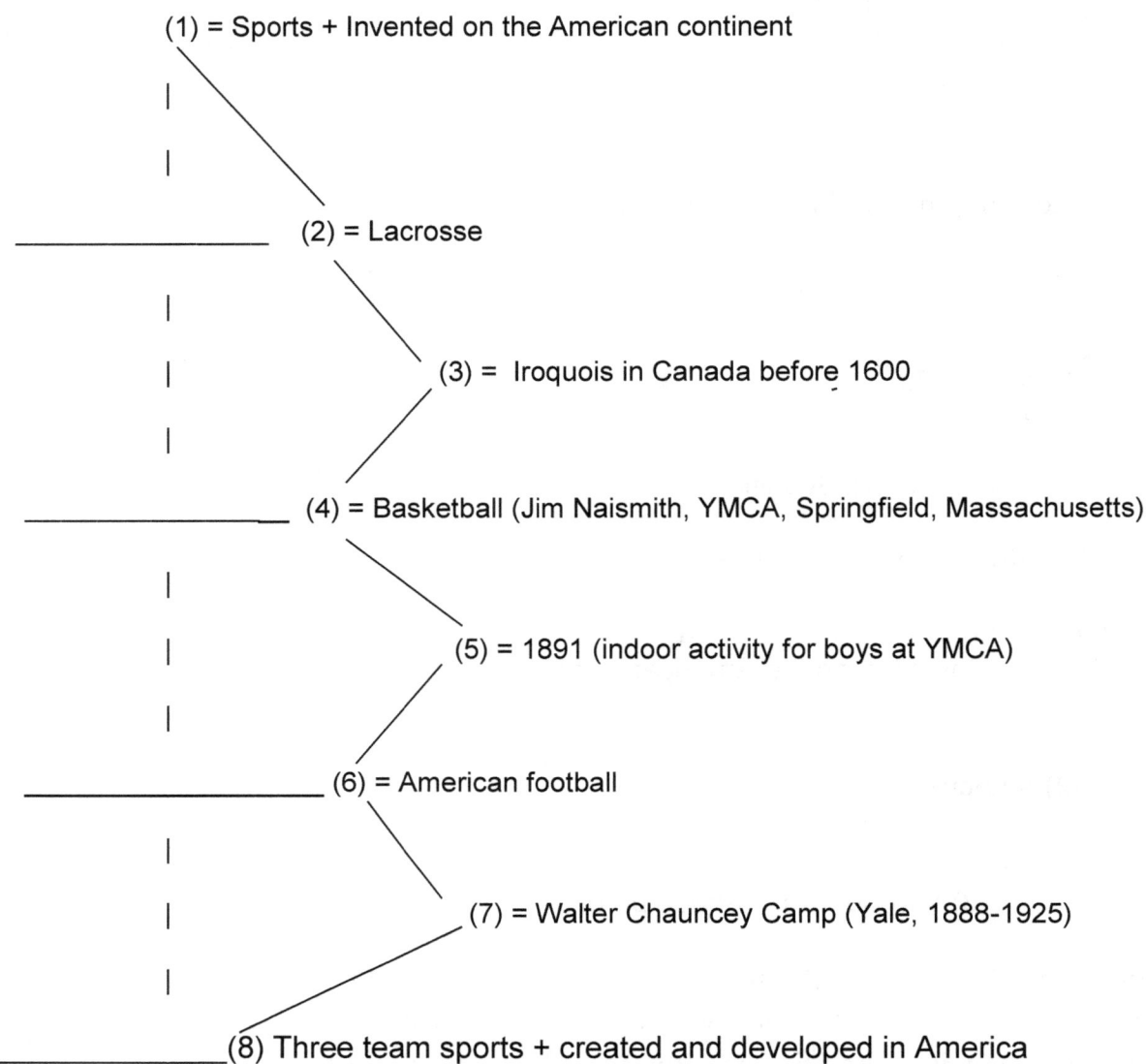

Notice the lines that connect the sentences. Do you see that they take a zigzag pattern? That is, the paragraph "zigs" and "zags" as it moves back and forth between points and details. For this reason, we will call it the *zigzag organization* of the English paragraph, or *zigzag paragraph* for short.

EXERCISE 4.4: Analyzing the Scheme

Directions: To firm these techniques in your memory, please do the following to the scheme on the previous page.

1. Put the letter G above the numbers 1 and 8 in the scheme. These numbers mark the GENERAL sentences.

2. Put the letter P above the numbers 2, 4, and 6 in the scheme. These numbers mark the POINTS.

3. Put the letter D above the numbers 3, 5, and 7 in the scheme. These numbers mark the DETAILS.

4. In the blanks to the left of Sentences 2, 4, 6, and 8, write the transition word that introduces the sentence.

EXERCISE 4.5: Analyzing "Zigzag" Paragraphs

Directions: Please begin by reading the sample paragraph. Then, working together as a class, answer the questions that follow.

Sightseeing in Boston

OLD NORTH CHURCH

(1) On our vacation to Boston last summer, our family visited three sites related to the American Revolution. (2) First, we went to the Old South Meeting House. (3) This is where the Boston Tea Party was planned and where the men probably put on their Mohawk costumes before heading down to the British ships in the harbor. (4) Second, we saw the Old State House, where the British had their quarters. (5) It was in front of the State House that the Boston Massacre began. (6) Third, we saw the Old North Church. (7) From the steeple of this church, men used lanterns to signal Paul Revere whether the British were coming by land (one lantern) or by sea (two lanterns). (8) In conclusion, if you ever want to tour Boston, you also might enjoy these three historic sites.

Questions:

1. Below you will see the scheme for "Sightseeing in Boston" Some parts of the scheme are shown, but others are not. Please complete the scheme by putting key words or phrases from the paragraph into the blanks. When finished, connect the numbers with the zigzag lines and insert the transitions.

        (1) = ___Family vacation to Boston___ + _____

_____ (2) = _____

        (3) = ___Where Boston Tea Party was planned___

_____ (4) = _____

        (5) = _____

_____(6) = ___Old North Church___

        (7) = _____

_____ (8) = _____ + ___three historic sites___

EXERCISE 4.6: Analyzing a "Zigzag" Paragraph

Directions: Please read the paragraph that follows. Then complete the scheme that follows by putting key words or phrases from the paragraph into the blanks. When finished, connect the numbers with the zigzag lines and insert the transitions.

Animal Names Borrowed from Native Americans

(1) When the English colonists in the New World encountered animals not found in Europe, they often adopted their Native American names. (2) One example from the northeastern part of the American continent is the word *moose*. (3) This word comes from the Algonquin word *moosu* ("he strips off"), a

reference to the moose's annual shedding of antlers. (4) Another example is the word *woodchuck*. (5) In this case, the colonists used the English words *wood* and *chuck* to represent the Algonquin word *wuchak*. (6) A third example is the word *coyote*. (7) This word comes from the Aztec word *coyotl*, pronounced as among Mexicans today, *kee-Ō-tee*. (8) In short, some of the names we use for animals on this continent were borrowed from the Native Americans.

(1) = _____  _____

_____ (2) = _____

(3) = _____

_____ (4) = _____

(5) = _____

_____ (6) = _____

(7) = _____

_____ (8) = _____ + _____

EXERCISE 4.7: Creating a Zigzag Scheme

Directions: Divide into small groups of three or four students. Then follow the steps below to create your own zigzag scheme.

1. Decide on one thing all members of your group have in common. You can choose from the list below or create your own topic.

   Possible Topics:

   a. Video games
   b. Dolls
   c. Pets
   d. Favorite food
   e. (Your choice)

2. The general topic will be *group members*. The controlling idea will be whatever you discover as the thing you have in common. Those will both appear beside the number 1, separated by a plus sign [+] (see schemes on previous pages).

3. Then go on to complete a zigzag scheme similar to the one at the right. (If you have a group of four students, add one more point and detail.)

4. After you have created your scheme, take it home and write up the paragraph. Be sure to include the listing signals (*first, second, third*, etc.) and a concluding sentence.

Quills: Zigzag Paragraph

The teacher will give you a list of topics. Choose a topic for which you can think of three points and a detail for each point. Prepare a zigzag scheme on a piece of notebook paper. Then write the paragraph, being sure to include the listing signals (*first, second, third*; or *one, another, another*) and a conclusion that begins with a transition (e.g., *in conclusion, in short*).

PROVERB AND CHREIA

Chapter 5

Introduction

> Blessed is the one who finds wisdom,
>   and the one who gets understanding,
> for the gain from her is better than gain from silver
>   and her profit better than gold.
> She is more precious than jewels,
>   and nothing you desire can compare with her.
> Long life is in her right hand;
>   in her left hand are riches and honor.
> Her ways are ways of pleasantness,
>   and all her paths are peace.
>
> Proverbs 3: 13-17

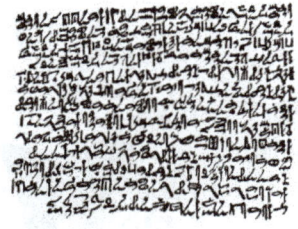

Papyrus with Maxims of Ptah-Hotep

One of the earliest forms of writing is called wisdom literature. In fact, the very first book ever written, *The Maxims of Ptah-Hotep*, was a collection of wise sayings written down by the Egyptian official Ptah-Hotep in 2500 BC. He wrote down wise sayings to help young people succeed in public service jobs.

In the Old Testament, the book of Proverbs is the wisdom literature of the Hebrew people, and in the New Testament, Paul wrote that Jesus "*became* to us wisdom from God" (1 Cor. 1:30) [emphasis added]. From these examples, we can see that passing on wisdom to the next generation has always been an important part of Jewish and Christian life.

Among the ancient teachers, the wisdom of the ages was presented in two forms: the Proverb and the Chreia. Both the Proverb and the Chreia can be about a wise saying, but a Chreia can also be about a wise action.

Because these two elements of the progymnasmata have many similarities, they have been put together in one chapter. As you go through the chapter, you will learn how to present the wisdom of the ancients to your friends, your family members, and even yourself!

 **THINK IT THROUGH:** From your own experiences, can you explain what truths the following proverbs teach about life?

- Early to bed and early to rise makes a man healthy, wealthy, and wise.
- Clean your finger before you point at my spots.
- Haste makes waste.

Part I: Proverb

Definition and Purpose of the Proverb

1. A *proverb* is a short statement that gives advice. Like the fable, the proverb is used to teach moral conduct. But unlike the fable, the proverb simply states the moral without leading up to it with a story.

2. The term *Expanded Proverb* refers to a composition or speech that explores the wisdom of a famous saying. By looking at a saying in multiple ways, we can come to understand it better and have a better chance of applying its truth in our own lives.

3. It is a common purpose of people everywhere to teach their children wisdom. In ancient, medieval, and modern times—in America, Europe, Asia, or Africa—people

have the same basic needs and emotions. Therefore, it is not surprising to find proverbs from different countries that have the same meaning, even though they may state the truth in different words.

 **THINK IT THROUGH:** What seems to be the common teaching about life in these pairs of proverbs?

Egyptian (Ptah-Hotep): "Silence is more profitable to you than abundance of speech."

German: "Talking is silver; silence is gold."

   Teaching: _____

English (Ben Franklin): "A penny saved is a penny earned."
Greek (Aesop): "Save for a rainy day."

   Teaching: _____

Bible: "The prudent sees danger and hides himself" (Proverbs 22:3a).
English: "Curiosity killed the cat."

   Teaching: _____

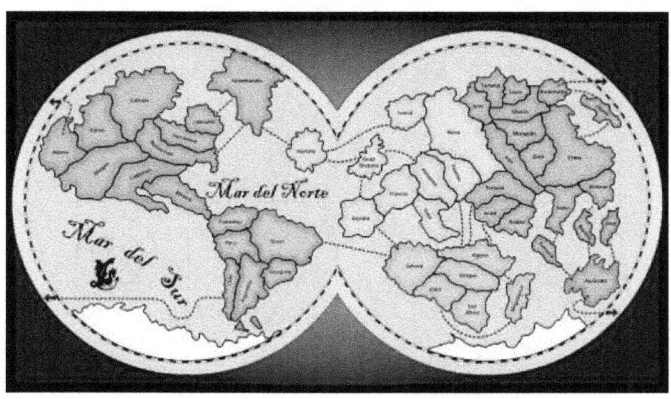

EXERCISE 5.1: Finding Proverbs of Similar Meaning

 Directions: In the exercise below, match the proverbs that have a similar meaning. Place the letter of one proverb in the blank of the matching proverb.

A. **Biblical:** A soft answer turns away wrath, but a harsh word stirs up anger (Proverbs 15:1).

B. **French:** Even a good fisherman may let an eel slip from him.

C. **Portuguese:** A house without either a cat or a dog is the house of a scoundrel.

D. **English:** All that glitters is not gold.

_____ 1. **English:** You catch more flies with honey than with vinegar.

_____ 2. **Italian:** Every glowworm is not a fire.

_____ 3. **American:** You can't win 'em all.

_____ 4. **American:** Never trust a person who doesn't love dogs.

Approaches to Proverb

A fully expanded Proverb has nine approaches. In this chapter, we will look at six of them.

Citation	Cite (or quote) the proverb.
Encomium	Praise the wisdom of our ancestors who gave us this observation about human life.
Paraphrase	Put the proverb into your own words.
Example	Give an example from fact or fiction of a person who acted in the manner taught by the proverb.
Testimony of the Ancients (Corroboration)	Quote an authority from the past to confirm the wisdom of the action.
Exhortation	Encourage your readers to exercise the wisdom of the proverb in their own lives.

Model Expanded Proverb

The Wisdom of Caution

Citation + Encomium

It was a wise person who cautioned, "Don't count your chickens before they hatch."

Paraphrase

This saying means that, as we plan for the future, we should not consider something to be certain before we have proof that it will indeed come to pass. After all, the farmer's wife may have breakfast plans for the eggs, so the hen cannot be certain all her eggs will hatch.

Example

What happened to my cousin Anna is an example of the wisdom of this saying. When Anna was fifteen, she applied for a job at a doggy day care center. On the day after she submitted her application, she began telling her friends and family that she was going to work at the center during the coming summer. However, in the end, the day care center did not hire her because they needed an employee who was at least sixteen. Anna was very embarrassed because now everyone knew that she had been turned down. She realized too late that she had "counted her chickens before they hatched."

Testimony of the Ancients

Proverbs 19:21 says, "Many are the plans in the mind of a man, but it is the purpose of the Lord that will stand." This teaching also tells us that we can make plans but we cannot always be sure they will come to pass. The Lord may have a different plan in mind for us.

Exhortation

    We are right to plan for the future, but at the same time we must realize that not every hope we have is actually going to come true. We must remain cautious until we are certain the plan will come to pass.

EXERCISE 5.2: Analyzing the Proverb about Caution

Directions: Please answer the questions below, which will help you analyze the model essay above entitled "The Wisdom of Caution."

1. In the first paragraph, underline the proverb that is being discussed and put squiggly lines under the part of the sentence that is "praise."

2. In the Paraphrase, the author says that this proverb means:

3. In one sentence summarize the example about fifteen-year-old Anna.

4. The author has briefly stated the Exhortation in the last sentence of the essay, which says we must:

Finding Proverbs and "Testimony of the Ancients"

You may have expressed an opinion in the past and some wag responded by saying, "Oh, yeah? Who says?" From a remark like this, we can see that a listener naturally seeks authority for what a speaker says.

This is why teachers from the earliest times have encouraged students to find support from a respected person. They called this technique "testimony of the ancients." Yes, it may be true that you think your teacher or parent is ancient, but the idea here is to choose the thoughts of someone who lived in the past and whose words have stood the test of time.

But how does a person go about finding who said what in the long ago? There are actually several resources that can help. The following exercises will direct you to two of them and provide you with some practice using them.

PLATO AND ARISTOTLE

EXERCISE 5.3: Finding Testimony of the Ancients on the Internet

Directions: Go to the *Topical Bible* web site on the Internet: <www.openbible.info/topics> . In the search bar, type a topic such as Animals, Prayer, or Forgiveness. Click Search. Then skim the verses that appear and choose one that you like. Write it in the space below, being sure to give the verse reference (such as John 3:16).

Topic: _____

Verse: _____

_____

Reference: _____

EXERCISE 5.4: Finding Proverbs on the Internet

Directions: In the Search Bar on your web browser, enter this Internet address: <www.bartleby.com/89>. This leads to the home page of a site entitled *Proverbs, Maxims, and Phrases of All Ages* compiled by Robert Christy. On the lower left side of the screen, you will see a list of topics. For each numbered item below, click on the topic and browse the sayings until you find one you like. Then copy it in the space provided.

1. Conscience

2. Honesty

3. Word

Quills #1: Expanded Proverb

 Your teacher will give you the instructions you need to write an Expanded Proverb.

Part II: Chreia

The tale of George Washington and the apple tree is familiar to most Americans. Mason Locke Weems—or Parson Weems, as he is usually called—recorded the story in 1800 in his book *The Life of Washington*. It goes this way:

> When George was about six years old, he was made the wealthy owner of a hatchet, of which, like most little boys, he was immoderately fond and was continually going about chopping everything that came in his way. One day in the garden where he often amused himself hacking his mother's pea sticks, he unluckily tried the edge of his hatchet on the body of a beautiful young English cherry tree, which he barked so terribly that I don't believe the tree ever got the better of it.
>
> The next morning, the old gentleman finding out what had befallen his tree, which, by the by, was a great favorite, came into the house and with much warmth asked for the mischievous author, declaring at the same time that he would not have taken five guineas for it.
>
> Presently George and his hatchet made their appearance. "George," said his father, "do you know who killed that beautiful little cherry tree yonder in the garden?" This was a tough question, and George staggered under it for a moment but quickly recovered himself and, looking at his father with the sweet face of youth brightened with the inexpressible charm of all conquering truth, he bravely cried out, "I can't tell a lie, Pa. You know I can't tell a lie. I did cut it with my hatchet."
>
> "Run to my arms, you dearest boy," cried his father in transports. "Run to my arms; glad am I, George, that you killed my tree, for you have paid me for it a thousand fold. Such an act of heroism in my son is worth more than a thousand trees though blossomed with silver and their fruits of purest gold."[21]

This short narrative is called a Chreia. In this chapter, you will learn its definition, purpose, and techniques.

Definition and Purpose of Chreia

a. The word *chreia* (pronounced KRAY-uh) is the Greek word for *anecdote*.

b. According to the Merriam-Webster dictionary, an anecdote is usually a "short narrative of an interesting, amusing, or biographical incident."[22]

c. The purpose of the progymnasmata exercise called Chreia is to explore the behavior of a wise or a foolish person so that readers or listeners can learn from the experience of others.

THINK IT THROUGH: What life lesson are we to learn from the anecdote about George Washington and the cherry tree?

THINK IT THROUGH: The purpose of many brief Bible narratives is to teach a moral lesson. With your classmates, discuss what you consider the teaching of each of these Biblical anecdotes:

- The good Samaritan (Luke 10:25-42)
- The lost sheep (Luke 15:3-7)
- The man who gave a great banquet (Luke14: 15-24)

Approaches to the Chreia

The approaches to the Chreia are quite similar to the approaches to the Proverb, as you can see in the chart below.

Narrative + Citation	Narrate the anecdote. If the anecdote includes a key quotation, include the quotation as well.

Encomium	Praise the person who chose the wise course of action.
Explanation	Explain what the person's action teaches us.
Example e.g.	Give an example from fact or fiction of a person who acted in the manner taught by the anecdote.
Testimony of the Ancients (Corroboration)	Quote an authority from the past to confirm the wisdom of the action.
Exhortation	Encourage your readers to exercise the wisdom of the anecdote in their own lives.

Exercise 5.5: Identifying Elements of Praise

Directions: Below are two narratives which can be considered historical anecdotes. After reading each, work together as a class to brainstorm approaches to the Chreia.

Rising to the Occasion

Have you ever felt that you were being asked to do something for which you were not quite prepared? That is the situation General Nathanael Greene found himself in during the Revolutionary War. Greene did not have the same level of education as other generals of the time.
Nathanael Greene
1742-1786

He could write clearly enough in an ordinary way, but he was not trained in the arts of rhetoric and persuasion. This became a problem in 1781 when there was a rebellion amongst some of his soldiers in the Hills of Santee in southwestern South Carolina. He had to write a letter to be read to the men, one that would calm them down and turn them back into reliable soldiers. Alexander Garden, who had brought him the news and who was going to carry the answer back to the complaining soldiers, was not sure that Greene was up to the task, but he noticed that Greene was writing energetically and feverishly tossing him the filled-up pages. However, before Garden returned to the rebels, he gave the letter to another general, just arrived in camp, to look over to make sure it was written well enough. Happily, the more educated general highly approved, saying, "I have never read a letter better calculated to produce the desired effect."[23] Greene came through in a pinch!

Questions:

1. **Narrative**

   a. **Who:** About whom is the narrative written?

   b. **When:** In what year did this event take place?

   c. **Where:** Where did the situation happen?

d. **What:** What had happened that required the general to write a letter?

e. **Why:** Why might this have caused a problem for the general?

f. **How:** What two *–ly* adverbs show how the general went about his task?

2. **Encomium:** What praise is due General Greene in this case?

3. **Explanation:** What do we learn from this anecdote?

4. **Example:** Cite a similar example that shows the same thing.

5. **Testimony of the Ancients:** What Bible verse, proverb, or famous quotation teaches the same thing?

6. **Exhortation:** What would you exhort your readers to do now that they know this anecdote?

Honoring Honesty

Gaspard de Coligny, Seigneur de Châtillon 1519-72

In the sixteenth century, the French admiral Châtillon [SHĂ-tee-yōn) went to hear mass in the Dominican Friars' chapel in Paris. A poor man came and begged his charity. Occupied with his devotions, Châtillon gave the man several pieces of gold from his pocket without counting them or thinking about what he was doing. The large amount astonished the beggar, and as the admiral was leaving the church, the poor man approached him. "Sir," he said, showing him the coins. "I cannot think that you intended to give me so large a sum, and am very ready to return it." The admiral, admiring the honesty of the man, said, "Indeed, my good man, I did not intend to have given you so much, but, since you have the generosity to offer to return it, I will have the generosity to desire you to keep it, and here are five pieces more for you."[24]

1. **Narrative**

    a. **Who:** About whom is this anecdote told?

    b. **When:** In what century did this event occur?

    c. **Where:** Where did this event occur?

    d. **What:** Briefly explain what Châtillon did when the poor man said that he (Châtillon) had given him too much money.

    e. **How:** How did Châtillon treat the poor man.

2. **Encomium:** What praise is due in this case?

3. **Explanation:** What do we learn from this anecdote?

4. **Example:** Cite a similar example that shows the same thing.

5. **Testimony of the Ancients:** What Bible verse, proverb, or famous quotation teaches the same thing?

6. **Exhortation:** What would you exhort your readers to do now that they know this?

Model Chreia

The Courage of Pocahontas

Narrative

In his book *The General History of Virginia,* the English explorer Captain John Smith (1580-1631) tells how he was captured by the Indians in 1607 and taken before Chief Powhatan. Since Smith could not speak the language of the natives, he was startled

by their dress and body paint, and he did not know if they meant him good or ill. Then one day after a feast, two great stones were brought before Powhatan, and a number of warriors took a hold of Smith and dragged him forward. They forced his head down onto the stones and were ready "with their clubs, to beate out his braines." Pocahontas, the eleven-year-old daughter of the chief, took pity on Smith and begged her father to spare his life. But when she realized the execution would go forward, she "got his head in her armes, and laid her owne upon his to save him from death." At that, Chief Powhatan released Smith, and relations with the Jamestown colony and the Powhatans improved for quite some time.[25]

Encomium (Praise)

Pocahontas showed great compassion and courage by her sudden action that day. It is no wonder that she has earned an honored position in American history.

Explanation

For over 400 years, this story has warmed people's hearts for two reasons. Not only was Pocahontas just a girl, but she risked her life to defend a stranger of a different race, whom her father may have considered an enemy.

Example

In some ways, Pocahontas' story is similar to Jesus' narrative about the Good Samaritan. The Samaritans and the Jews were not friendly with each other, but when a Jewish man was beaten and robbed on the highway, no one would stop to help him except the Samaritan, his traditional enemy.

Testimony of the Ancients

Jesus himself talked about taking risks for others when he said, "Greater love has no one than this, that someone lay down his life for his friends" (John 15:13).

Exhortation

In the next verse, John records that Jesus also said, "You are my friends if you do what I command you." Therefore, though it takes great courage, let us follow Pocahontas' example and be strong to protect the lives of others.

EXERCISE 5.6: Analyzing a Chreia

Directions: Analyze the Chreia about Pocahontas by answering the following questions.

1. In the Narrative, what did Pocahontas do to save Captain Smith?

2. In the Encomium, the writer praised Pocahontas for what virtue?

3. In the Explanation, the writer explains that people have long found this story meaningful for two reasons:

   a. _____

   b. _____

4. In the Example, what Bible narrative is used as an example of the same virtues?

5. In Testimony of the Ancients, whose words are quoted to support Pocahontas' actions?

6. In the Exhortation, what are we encouraged to do?

EXERCISE 5.7: Paraphrasing Practice

Directions: Below are some famous quotations. In the space provided, write a paraphrase of the quotation. The first one serves as an example.

1. "A house divided against itself cannot stand"
   (Abraham Lincoln, paraphrasing Mark 3:25)

   A country will be ruined if there is serious division among its people.

2. "It is easier to prevent bad habits than to break them" (Benjamin Franklin).

3. "The stronger the wind, the stronger the trees" (William Marriott).

4. "Gratitude is the fairest blossom which springs from the soul" (Henry Ward Beecher).

5. "I know it is wet and the sun is not sunny, but we can have lots of good fun that is funny" (Dr. Seuss, *The Cat in the Hat*).

6. (Speaking of Jesus): "He must increase, I must decrease" (John 3:30).

Quills #2: Chreia

 Your teacher will give you the instructions you need to write a Chreia.

ENCOMIUM AND INVECTIVE

Chapter 6

The following excerpt is from *Travels with a Donkey in the Cévennes* by the Scottish author, Robert Louis Stevenson. Touring through the French countryside with a donkey in 1879 was not always easy, and Modestine (for that was the donkey's name) gave Stevenson more than a bit of trouble. However, as he left the town of Cheylard, he had this to say about another nagging issue:

A 21st-century traveler following Stevenson's route through the Cévennes

It was not only heavy thoughts about Modestine that weighted me upon the way; it was a leaden business altogether. For first, the wind blew so rudely that I had to hold on the pack with one hand from Cheylard to Luc; and second, my road lay through one of the most beggarly countries in the world. It was like the worst of the Scottish Highlands, only worse; cold, naked, and ignoble, scant of wood, scant of heather, scant of life. A road and some fences broke the unvarying waste, and the line of the road was marked by upright pillars, to serve in time of snow.[26]

But not everything about the region was so unappealing. Near Monastier, Stevenson wrote this:

The stony skeleton of the world was here vigorously displayed to sun and air. The slopes were steep and changeful. Oak-trees clung along the hills, well grown, wealthy in leaf, and touched by the autumn with strong and luminous colours. Here and there another stream would fall in from the right or the left, down a gorge of snow-white and tumultuary boulders. The river in the bottom . . . here foamed a while in desperate rapids, and there lay in pools of the most enchanting sea-green shot with watery browns. As far as I have gone, I have never seen a river of so changeful and delicate a hue: crystal was not more clear. . . .[27]

What we see here is that, like many travelers, Stevenson encountered both the ugly and the beautiful. And, like most of us, he scorns the ugly and praises the beautiful. In classical composition, the scorning parts are called Invective. The praising parts are called Encomium. The purpose of this chapter is to introduce the techniques of Encomium and Invective and give you a chance to practice them.

Definitions and Purposes of Encomium and Invective

An *encomium* is a composition or a speech whose purpose is to offer praise.

An *invective* is a composition or a speech whose purpose is to offer blame.

THINK IT THROUGH:

From your study of history, what people do you consider worthy to receive a composition or speech of praise? Why?

THINK IT THROUGH:

From your study of history, what people do you think deserve public criticism (or blame)?

Subjects and Occasions of Encomium and Invective

In our day and age, we still use Encomium and Invective. Some examples are listed below.

Occasions for Encomium (Praise)

- Funerals
- Wedding receptions
- Nominations for political office
- Awards ceremonies
- Retirement parties

Occasions for Invective (Blame)

- Commentary in the media about an evil-doer (e.g., tyrant, assassin, terrorist)
- Sermons about Biblical figures or groups who committed evil
- Speech to a jury about a murderer who deserves punishment

 **THINK IT THROUGH:**

a. Tell the class about a time you heard someone praise another person publicly.

b. Tell the class about a time you heard someone speak out against another person publicly.

Approaches to Encomium and Invective

Full-length Encomia and Invectives have five approaches. In this chapter, we will focus on three of them: background, character (virtues or vices), and deeds (good or evil).

Approach	Explanation
Background + Narrative	Introduce the person by telling his/her parents, place of birth, education, and other things that help us understand the person.
Character	**In Encomium:** Tell the person's *virtues*: loyalty, faith, fair-mindedness, helpfulness, etc.
	In Invective: Tell the person's *vices*: drug-addiction, cruelty, injustice, double-dealing, anger, etc.
Deeds	**In Encomium:** Tell the person's specific achievements: heroic acts, exploration, discovery, awards, etc.
	In Invective: Tell the person's specific evil deeds: treachery, murder, acts of cruelty, bullying, robbery, etc.

Student Text

Part I: Encomium

EXERCISE 6.1: Encomium Statements

<u>Directions</u>: Below are some examples of encomium-like statements from various books. Read each one and determine whether the statement refers to (a) a good character trait or (b) a good deed. Place the letter of the correct answer in the corresponding blank.

A. Good character traits
B. Good deeds

_____ 1. **Narrative:** *Betsy Ross was a resident of colonial Philadelphia who is credited with making the first American flag. The story is told that General George Washington, who desired a flag with stars representing the colonies, originally suggested a six-pointed star, thinking it would be easier to make. However, Betsy suggested that a five-pointed star would look better and promptly picked up her scissors to show how easily she could make one. Her design was approved by Congress, and she was asked to make as many flags as she could. Her grandson, William J. Canby, made the statement below in 1870.*

Encomium: "As an example of industry, energy and perseverance, and of humble reliance upon providence, through all the trials, which were not few, of her eventful life, the name of Elizabeth [Ross] Claypoole is worthy of being placed on record for the benefit of those who should be similarly circumstanced. Not only did she conduct with ability and skill her arduous business, but she was one of those women, whose hearts, like the magnet to its pole, always turned towards poverty, sickness and sorrow, and lent itself to the alleviations of every distress till she became, amongst her neighbors, like a kind shepherdess amidst her sheep, looked up to and beloved by all"[28] (William J. Canby).

_____ 2. **Narrative:** *Anthony Ashley-Cooper, the 7th Earl of Shaftesbury (1801-1885), was a member of the English House of Lords. A Christian man, he was devoted to helping the poor, especially poor children, in Victorian England. After establishing numerous schools, called Ragged Schools, for*

Encomium and Invective | 83

the instruction of London's street children, he turned his attention to the terrible housing conditions in which they lived. As a result, Parliament passed an act requiring government inspection and improvement of the "repulsive" lodging houses where many orphans lived.

Encomium: "To Lord Shaftesbury's legislation, we owe the gratifying fact that these recesses [lodgings] are explored by authorised [*sic*] persons, that houses are no longer permitted to take in more than as many as can breathe properly in them, that lodging in cellars is prohibited, that the rooms are properly cleaned and whitewashed, that ventilation, lighting, and drainage are provided for, and the furniture of the houses sufficient for the authorised number of lodg'ers"[29] (*London Times*).

_____ 3. **Narrative:** *George Richard Jesse was a zoophilist (animal lover) and defender of animals in England in the 1800's. Just as people in England had spoken up against the slave trade, he felt obliged to speak up for animals. In 1875, he appeared before the British Parliament to advocate against the cruel treatment of animals. Earlier, in 1866, he had written a book about the history of the British dog. The quote below is from that book's opening page.*

Encomium: "Of all animals, the dog appeals most strongly to the hearts of human beings. It is the dog that by feeling, instinct, and education can best appreciate our care, our love. Take the dog in the aggregate, weigh him against ourselves in moral qualities such as patience, trustfulness, unselfishness—has he not often proved an example to shame man? How frequently the brute is our superior. If the world fail, you go home, and if you have a dog, there you will find a friend ever to be depended on. How many unhappy beings in neglect and solitude pass their hands fondly over the coats of their sympathizing dumb [silent] companions and say (perhaps unconsciously), '*You* will never leave me nor desert me!'"[30]

Organization: Writing a Conclusion

Just as a stand-alone paragraph needs a brief concluding sentence, an essay needs a brief concluding paragraph. In this chapter, you will have the opportunity to examine and practice two popular techniques for writing a conclusion.

The first technique is summary. The second is the use of a quotation. It is even possible to use both techniques together and still have a paragraph of only two sentences. As you read the model Encomium and the model Invective, you will have a chance to look more closely at techniques for conclusions.

Model Encomium

A Tribute to William Bradford

Background + Narrative

William Bradford (c. 1590-1657) was an English Puritan who came to the American continent on the *Mayflower* in 1620. Before coming to America, he had been among those Puritans who decided to separate from England and move to Holland in order to have religious freedom. .After a few years in Holland, these Separatists decided to move to the New World, where they founded Plymouth Colony. In 1621, William Bradford became governor of Plymouth colony.

Character

William Bradford had several character traits that helped the Plymouth colonists succeed. First, he was a man of faith. Despite all the troubles the pilgrims had in the New World, Bradford encouraged them always to "praise the Lord because he is good, and his mercies endure forever."[31] Second, he was courageous. When the *Mayflower* arrived on the shores of the New World, Bradford volunteered to lead some of the men on an expedition on shore while the others waited safely on board the ship. Third, as the Bible advises leaders to do, he always sought advice from others before making decisions. He especially valued the advice of Miles Standish on any military matters that faced the pilgrims.

Achievements

Bradford had several notable achievements. First, he was elected governor five times, serving from 1621 to 1657. Second, despite the fact that he had a limited education, he wrote the history called *Of Plymouth Plantation*. One scholar referred to him as "a story-teller of considerable power."[32] Third, when the pilgrims were struggling from lack of food, Bradford, with the advice of others, decided they could improve their crop yield if each family farmed its own parcel of land. Since this experiment was very successful, Bradford's system of private enterprise became the foundation of the American way of life.

Conclusion

In short, Governor William Bradford was a godly, courageous, and humble leader who helped the pilgrims survive many hardships and establish a way of life for generations of Americans to come.

EXERCISE 6.2: Analyzing an Encomium

Directions: Analyze the essay entitled "A Tribute to William Bradford" by answering the questions below.

1. What do we learn about William Bradford in Background + Narrative?

    a. Nationality: _____

    b. Religion: _____

    c. Year he came to America: _____

    d. Elected office in Plymouth Colony: _____

2. What three character traits (virtues) are given in Character?

    a. He was a man of _____.

    b. He was _____.

    c. He sought _____.

3. Answer these questions about the section called Achievements.

   a. How many times was Bradford elected governor?

   b. What was the title of his famous book?

   c. What did he do to solve the food shortage in the colony?

4. Which of the following is true of the Conclusion?

   A. It introduces one more virtue.

   B. It introduces one more achievement.

   C. It summarizes the virtues and the achievements.

Quills #1: Encomium

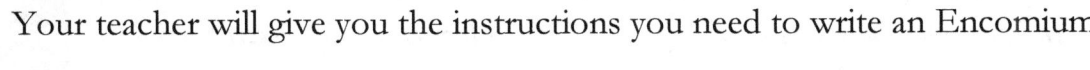
Your teacher will give you the instructions you need to write an Encomium.

Part II: Invective

Whereas an encomium focuses on a person's good traits and good deeds, an invective focuses on his or her bad traits or bad deeds. But what exactly is the difference between a *trait* and a *deed*? A trait is a quality or characteristic that belongs to a person. For example, you might say that your friend is *kind* or *athletic*. But the person's deeds are the actions that he or she does. For example, a kind person may help an elderly person with a grocery cart, or an athletic person might score the most points in a basketball game. The exercise below will focus on the difference between character traits and deeds.

EXERCISE 6.3: Invective Statements

Directions: Below are some examples of invective statements in today's media. Read each one and determine whether the statement refers to bad character traits or bad deeds. Place the letter of the correct answer in the corresponding blank.

> A. Bad character traits
> B. Bad deeds

____ 1. **Narrative:** *In 1776, the quarrels between the American colonies and the English king, George III, became more than just a series of quarrels. The colonists decided to break with England and wrote out a list of their reasons for seeking independence. This document, which is called the Declaration of Independence, was signed on July 4, 1776. Here is a brief excerpt from the Declaration, in which the colonists list some of their grievances against the king.*

George III

Invective: HE has combined with others to subject us to a Jurisdiction foreign to our Constitution, and unacknowledged by our Laws; giving his Assent to their Acts of pretended Legislation:
- o FOR quartering large Bodies of Armed Troops among us:
- o FOR protecting them, by a mock Trial, from Punishment for any Murders which they should commit on the Inhabitants of these States:
- o FOR cutting off our Trade with all Parts of the World:
- o FOR imposing Taxes on us without our Consent:
- o FOR depriving us, in many Cases, of the Benefits of Trial by Jury. . . .

Student Text

____ 2. **Narrative:** *1 Samuel 21-22 tells what happened when David fled the wrath of King Saul. He showed up in Nob and spoke with the priest Ahimelech. Keeping his escape a secret, he led the priest to believe that the king had sent him on a mission. He then asked for food and a weapon. Ahimelech gave him some of the consecrated bread and the sword that had belonged to Goliath. David was not aware that Doeg the Edomite, Saul's chief shepherd, was secretly observing this meeting. Later, Doeg told the king that Ahimelech had aided David. Unfortunately, he did not tell the whole truth; he did not tell the king that the priest was unaware that David was on the run. Furious, Saul ordered the deaths of all the priests of Nob, eighty-five in all, including the innocent Ahimelech. David later wrote about Doeg the Edomite in a psalm.*

Doeg the Edomite kills Ahimelech.

Invective:

¹ Why do you boast of evil, O mighty man?
   The steadfast love of God endures all the day.
² Your tongue plots destruction,
   like a sharp razor, you worker of deceit.
³ You love evil more than good,
   and lying more than speaking what is right. *Selah*
⁴ You love all words that devour,
   O deceitful tongue.

                    Psalm 52:1-4

____ 3. **Narrative:** *Benedict Arnold was an American general during the Revolutionary War, who committed treason by conspiring to turn West Point over to the British. His name has almost become a synonym for* traitor.

Invective: "Arnold's pride led him to switch to the British side because he felt he was not promoted quick [sic] enough and was not getting the credit he deserved. Also just as much as his pride led him to switch sides, so did his money problems. Arnold incurred much debt while he recuperated from his leg wound and if the plan at West Point had been successful Arnold would have been paid nicely for his treachery"³³ (Justin Barr).

Model Invective

An Invective against King Saul

Background + Narrative

Saul was the first king of Israel. The people had demanded that God give them a king, and though God warned them they would rue the day they took a king, they insisted that they wanted to be like other nations and needed a king. God gave them Saul. As God had foretold, Saul's kingship brought disaster on Israel.

Vices

Saul had three great vices. First, he was very jealous. In particular, he was jealous of David, whom the Lord had chosen to replace him. Secondly, he was disobedient to the Lord. The Lord asked Saul for total obedience, but Saul gave only partial obedience. This disobedience led to his third vice: his murderous heart. Because Saul was disobedient, the Lord withdrew his own Spirit from Saul and put in its place an evil spirit to torment him. Soon after, we see a third vice: Saul flew into murderous rages.

Evil Deeds

Because of his jealousy and his evil spirit, Saul committed evil deeds. He set out to kill David, who had saved Israel from the Philistines by killing Goliath and who had done Saul no wrong. Then, when Saul's son Jonathan, David's friend, tried to soften his father's heart, Saul heaved his spear at him in anger. In the end, he poured out this murderous rage on himself.

Death of Saul
By Gustave Doré

As the Philistines prepared to attack, Saul was still not willing to repent and trust the Lord. Instead, he committed suicide by falling on his own sword.

Conclusion

Saul, the first king of Israel, was a sinful man. He was jealous and disobedient. He was given over to an evil spirit and, in the end, had not victory, but death.

EXERCISE 6.4: Analyzing an Invective

Directions: Analyze the essay entitled "An Invective against Saul" by answering the questions below.

1. In Background + Narrative:

   a. Saul is identified as a _____ of _____.

   b. How did it come to pass that God gave Israel a king?

3. In Character, what three bad character traits (vices) are named?

   a. _____

   b. _____

   c. _____

4. In Evil Deeds, what three evil deeds are mentioned?

   a. _____

   b. _____

   c. _____

5. True or False? The conclusion is a summary of points from the essay.

Quills #2: Invective

 Your teacher will give you the instructions you need to write an Invective.

REFUTATION AND CONFIRMATION

Chapter 7

Introduction

The Adventures of Pinocchio (1883) by the Italian author Carlo Collodi tells the story of a poor woodcarver named Gepetto, who carves a marionette from a special block of wood and names him Pinocchio, which means "pine eye." Treating Pinocchio as his own son, Gepetto sends the "boy" to school, but on the way, Pinocchio sells a schoolbook in order to buy a theater ticket. One bad decision leads to another until Pinocchio finds himself with five gold coins (intended for his father) and a predicament from which he is rescued by a Fairy. In Chapter 17, we see Pinocchio's greed get the better of him. It begins when the Fairy starts asking him questions:

"Where are the gold pieces now?" the Fairy asked.

"I lost them," answered Pinocchio, but he told a lie, for he had them in his pocket.

As he spoke, his nose, long though it was, became at least two inches longer.

"And where did you lose them?"

"In the wood near by."

At this second lie, his nose grew a few more inches.

"If you lost them in the near-by wood," said the Fairy, "we'll look for them and find them, for everything that is lost there is always found."

"Ah, now I remember," replied the Marionette, becoming more and more confused. "I did not lose the gold pieces, but I swallowed them when I drank the medicine."

At this third lie, his nose became longer than ever, so long that he could not even turn around. If he turned to the right, he knocked it against the bed or into the windowpanes; if he turned to the left, he struck the walls or the door; if he raised it a bit, he almost put the Fairy's eyes out.

The Fairy sat looking at him and laughing.

"Why do you laugh?" the Marionette asked her, worried now at the sight of his growing nose.

"I am laughing at your lies."

"How do you know I am lying?"

"Lies, my boy, are known in a moment. There are two kinds of lies, lies with short legs and lies with long noses. Yours, just now, happen to have long noses."

Pinocchio, not knowing where to hide his shame, tried to escape from the room, but his nose had become so long that he could not get it out of the door.

Don't you wish that it was always so easy to determine when a person is lying? Unfortunately, in the real world, it is much more difficult to determine whether someone is telling the truth or not. In order to establish the truth of a matter in a court of law, lawyers, in their training, learn time-tested methods that help determine the truth.

One of the main purposes of a classical education is to prepare citizens for life in a republic, and since courtrooms are very much a part of a democracy, it is not surprising that students in ancient times were given skills to help them become truth detectors. In this chapter, you will be introduced to these skills and will be given an opportunity to practice them.

Definition and Purpose

When people try to prove that something is not true, they *refute* it. The process is called a *refutation*. When people try to prove that something is true, they *confirm* it. The process is called a *confirmation*.

The purpose of Refutation is to point out weaknesses in a person's narrative of events. The purpose of Confirmation is to point out the strengths in a person's narrative.

THINK IT THROUGH:

- Narrate for your classmates a time when you were fairly certain someone was not telling the truth. What made you suspicious?

- Narrate a time when you were certain someone was innocent and were able to come to his or her defense.

Approaches to Refutation and Confirmation

When trying to prove or disprove the truth of a narrative, there are four basic questions you can ask:

Is the narrative:

- possible or impossible?
- probable or improbable?
- clear or unclear?
- consistent or inconsistent?

The chart below provides explanations and examples for these four approaches.

Possible or Impossible?

Here you want to ask if the event is possible according to the laws of nature.

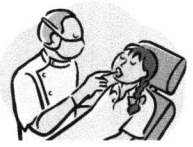

Example: If Agatha was at the dentist's office when something was stolen from her classmate's locker, Agatha could not have been the thief because it would be impossible for her to be in two places at the same time.

Probable or Improbable?

Here you want to ask if the events are too unusual to have happened. In other words, did the event *probably* happen in a certain way.

Example: Since we cannot be 100% sure if there is life on other planets, we might conclude it is *possible* that space aliens landed in New Mexico, but such an event would certainly be very unusual. Many people would argue that it *probably* did not happen. In other words, the narrative is improbable.

Clear or Unclear?

Here you want to determine whether the facts of the case are clear or not.

Example: If Charlie reports that somebody beat him up but cannot tell the police when or where the attack happened, then obviously the facts are not clear. This might lead police to believe the narrative is not true.

Consistent or Inconsistent?

Here you want to find out if there are any contradictions in the story.

Example: Suppose while the Millers are on vacation, Gillie is being paid to water their plants. When they arrive home, the plants have all died. Gillie, however, says that he watered the plants every day. Then later he says he watered them on Monday and Wednesday. Then later he says he watered them on Thursday. Since the story keeps changing, the neighbors might suspect Gillie is not telling the truth. His story is inconsistent.

EXERCISE 7.1: Truth-Detecting

Below are some narratives of criminal cases that have made the news. Using the above chart to guide you, determine with your classmates whether you think the narrative would be easier for police to refute or to confirm.

1. In 2011, a teenager (whom we will call Jack) stole several items from Marc Fisher, a journalist who writes for the *Washington Post,* including some clothing and a laptop

belonging to Fisher's son, whom we will call Kip. Shortly thereafter, Kip's friends noticed that on his (Kip's) Facebook timeline, Jack had posted a picture of himself wearing one of the items of clothing he had stolen from Mr. Fisher. From the photo, the police were able to discover Jack's identity and make an arrest.

a. What elements of the story make it seem *possible* or *impossible* that Jack was the robber? Explain your answer.

b. What elements make it seem *probable* or *improbable* that Jack was the thief? Explain your answer.

c. What elements make it *clear* or *unclear* that Jack was the thief?

d. Are the facts of the case *consistent* or *inconsistent*? Explain your answer.

2. A family in Houston, Texas, owned a small dog named Honey, who went missing one day. By reviewing video from a surveillance camera installed at their home, they discovered what appeared to be the "dognapping" of Honey. A woman wearing a pink pantsuit stopped her car in front of the family's house. The dog could be seen running in the street toward the woman. The woman picked up the dog, walked around a bit, then put the dog in the car and drove off. The woman in the pink suit was not identified. After the family posted fliers in the neighborhood, they received a phone call from a person who threatened to kill the dog. What does this narrative suggest to you?

a. Is it *possible* or *impossible* that the woman in the pink pantsuit kidnapped (or, dognapped) Honey? That she made the phone call? Explain your answers.

b. Is it *probable* or *improbable* that the woman took the dog? That she made the phone call? Explain your answers.

c. Is it *clear* or *unclear* that the woman actually kidnapped the dog, or is there another explanation? Explain your answer.

3. At 4 a.m. on a snowy night in 2014, a man named Victor, who lived in Massapequa, New York, entered a Dunkin' Donuts restaurant at 4 a.m. He selected a donut and tried to pay for it with a credit card, but the card was declined by the bank. He then pointed a gun at the store's employee and demanded money. After the employee handed him some money, Victor fled the store on foot. When police arrived, they took down a description of the thief and then noticed a fresh set of footprints in the heavily falling snow. They followed the footsteps to a nearby house, where they discovered Victor, a man who resembled the description given by the employee. They later learned that Victor was the owner of the home. In Victor's possession was the stolen credit card he had tried to use at Dunkin' Donuts. Victor was arrested and charged with robbery, possession of a weapon, and criminal use of a firearm.

   a. Is it *possible* or *impossible* that Victor was the thief? Explain your answer.

   b. Is it *probable* or *improbable* that Victor was the thief? Explain your answer.

   c. Is it *clear* or *unclear* that Victor was the thief? Explain your answer.

   d. Is there anything about the story that is *inconsistent* with the employee's report to the police? Explain your answer.

Organizing a Refutation or Confirmation

Below is the organization pattern for a composition of this type.

1. Narrative	Here you narrate the events that you are going to discuss. <ul><li>For example, in a court of law, the lawyer would lay out for the jury the story of what happened.</li></ul>
2. Your Opinion	Here you indicate your opinion about what happened. <ul><li>For example, in a court of law, the prosecutor would say the defendant was guilty, while the defense would say the defendant was not guilty.</li></ul>
3. Approaches 1st 2nd 3rd 4th	Use the four approaches to show that the narrative was: <ul><li>Possible or Impossible</li><li>Probable or Improbable</li><li>Clear or Unclear</li><li>Consistent or Inconsistent</li></ul>These can be used in any order. Also, if one of them is not related to your topic, you do not have to use it.
4. Conclusion	Write a brief statement restating your opinion and recapping the approaches you used.

Model Confirmation <u>Directions</u>: Below is a model composition entitled "The Riddle of the Sphinx." After reading the composition, proceed to "What To Notice."

The Riddle of the Sphinx

Narrative

The sphinx was a mythical creature of the ancient world. It had the body of a lion, but the head of a man. It was said to stand guard at the ancient city of Thebes, and anyone wanted to enter Thebes had to answer the riddle of the sphinx: "Which creature speaks with one voice and walks on four legs in the morning, two legs in the afternoon, and three legs in the evening?" The sphinx would gobble up any person who could not answer the riddle.

Writer's Opinion

I believe the riddle describes a human being. In the "morning" of life, a baby crawls on all fours (hands and knees). In the "afternoon" of life, a person walks upright on two legs. In the "evening" of life, a person often walks with a cane, the third "leg" of the riddle.

Clear

First, it is *clear* the riddle is describing a person because only a person can speak. Other animals can make sounds, but only people speak.

Possible

Also, it is very *possible* the creature is a person because people are the only creatures who walk upright on two legs. An ape can walk on its two legs but has very long arms which assist in walking. Only a human can walk when completely upright.

Probable

Next, it is *probable* the riddle refers to a person because only people use canes.

Consistent

Last, every part of the riddle is *consistent* with the way humans move at three different stages of life: infancy, maturity, and old age. Also, the reference to speaking is also consistent with the characteristics of a human.

Conclusion

For these reasons, it is *possible, probable, clear,* and *consistent* that the riddle is describing a human being.

EXERCISE 7.2: Analyzing a Confirmation

1. **Introduction:** The Narrative has two parts:

    a. An explanation of _____

    b. A statement of _____

2. **List Words:** Starting with the paragraph entitled "Clear," the first word in each paragraph serves to list the points. Write down the listing word from each paragraph. The first one serves as an example

    *First*_____ _____ _____ _____

3. **Key Words:** In the first sentence of each paragraph (the topic sentence), there is a key word in italics. It tells the topic of the paragraph. Write the key words in the blanks below. The first one serves as an example.

    *Clear*_____ _____ _____ _____

4. **Wrapping Up:** What is the content of the conclusion?

EXERCISE 7.3: Practice Approaches to Refutation and Confirmation

Directions: For this exercise, break into small groups. Then work together to solve the riddles below. By looking at the clues in the riddle, see if you can figure out what is being described. In both cases, remember to approach the puzzle by considering whether your solution is possible, probable, clear, and consistent.

Riddle #1

From the *Exeter Book* (10th-century England)

What Am I?

A moth ate words.   To me it seemed,
A remarkable fate,   when I learned of the wonder,
That the worm had swallowed,   the speech of a man,
A thief in the night,   a renowned saying,
And its place itself,   Though he swallowed the word,
The thieving stranger   was no whit the wiser.[34]

Riddle #2

What Am I?

There's not a kingdom on the earth,
But I have travell'd o'er and o'er,
And though I know not whence my birth,
Yet when I come, you know my roar.

I through the town do take my flight,
And through the fields and meadows green,
And whether it be day or night,
I neither am nor can be seen.

Quills #1

Choose your solution to either Riddle #1 or Riddle #2 and write a Confirmation, proving your solution is correct. Use the four approaches: Possible, Probable, Clear, and Consistent. Follow the pattern of the model composition explaining the cat riddle.

Model Refutation Essay

Henry Sinclair, Earl of Orkney, Did Not Discover America

Narrative

Since the sixteenth century, various writers have claimed that America was discovered between 1380 and 1398 by a Scotsman named Henry Sinclair, 1st Earl of Orkney, supposedly traveling with two navigators from Venice: Nicolo Zeno and his brother Antonio. In 1996 a monument to Sinclair's expedition was even raised in the Canadian province of Nova Scotia (Latin for *New Scotland*). The various writers who have made the claim base their work on letters written by Nicolo Zeno of Venice around 1400. Zeno's writings state that he and his brother accompanied a leader named Zichmni in his

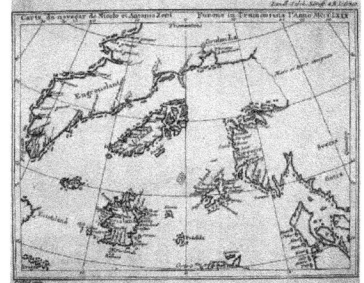
The Zeno Map

campaign against warlords on several islands in the North Atlantic near Greenland and Iceland. He included maps along with his text in order to show exactly where they traveled with Zichmni.

Writer's Opinion

Though several authors have tried to make a case that Henry Sinclair discovered America more than a hundred years before Columbus, a historian named Brian Smith has shown how this cannot be true.

Unclear

First, Smith points out that it is very *unclear* that the person Nicolo Zeno called Zichmni was actually Henry Sinclair. In fact, Zeno never actually referred to anyone called Sinclair. Furthermore, Zeno never stated that Sinclair and the Zeno brothers ever reached America. Rather, Zeno claimed Zichmni went to Greenland.

Improbable

Second, Smith shows it is *improbable* that Henry Sinclair discovered America. No claim about Sinclair making such a marvelous discovery was ever made during his lifetime. In fact, it was 500 years before anyone claimed that Sinclair was the person called Zichmni in the Zeno letters. If he had discovered a world previously unknown in Europe, someone would probably have reported it to the king or written about it in a letter. Since nothing of this type has been found, we can say that the event probably never happened.

Inconsistent

Next, Smith points out that one of the authors making the claim about Sinclair has been inconsistent in the way he has interpreted Nicolo Zeno's writings. For example, Frederick Pohl said in 1950 that *Zichmni* was a miswriting of the name Sinclair. Then, in 1974, he said that *Zichmni* referred to the phrase *d'Orkney (of Orkney)*, which he said proved that Zichmni was Henry Sinclair, the earl of Orkney. These two explanations are not consistent.

Impossible

Last, Smith shows that the voyage Zeno described would have been impossible. To be specific, Zeno said the expeditioners visited islands called Frislanda, Talas, Broas, Iscant, Trans, Mimant, Dambert, and Bres. He even put these places on his map. However, these islands have never existed, nor have the imaginary countries of Estotilanda and Drogeo, which Zeno also mentioned. Since these places have never existed, Henry Sinclair could never have visited them. Moreover, America does not appear on the map at all, so it is impossible to conclude that Sinclair landed in America on the voyage Zeno described.

Conclusion

In short, the stories that claim Henry Sinclair, 1st earl of Orkney, waged war in the north Atlantic and discovered America on the way are improbable, unclear, inconsistent, and even impossible. Therefore, they should be considered untrue.

EXERCISE 7.4: Analyzing a Refutation

1. **Introduction:** The first paragraph provides the narrative about Henry Sinclair's supposed discovery of America. Fill in the blanks in order to provide the elements of the narrative: Who, What, When, Where, Why, and How.

   According to the information in the Narrative, a Scotsman named _____ _____ discovered _____ sometime between the years _____ and _____. However, the original narrative was not about the Scotsman, but about an adventurer named _____. The original narrative was written by _____ in about _____. According to the original narrative, the adventurer was _____ islands in the _____ Ocean. Along with his story, the original author included _____ in order to show where _____ _____.

Student Text

2. **Writer's Opinion:** Does the writer of the model essay agree or disagree about Henry Sinclair's discovery?

3. **Unclear:** According to the writer of the model essay, what is not clear?

4. **Improbable:** Why does the writer of the model essay say it is improbable that Henry Sinclair discovered America before 1400?

5. **Inconsistent:** What inconsistency does the writer point out?

6. **Impossible:** What two reasons does the writer of the model essay provide to prove that it is impossible for Sinclair to have conducted the voyage Zeno described?

    a. _____

    b. _____

7. **Conclusion:** In the conclusion, underline the four words that recap the four approaches used in the essay.

8. **Organization:** Underline the transition that begins each of the approaches and the conclusion.

Applying Confirmation and Refutation to Literature

"Innocent until proven guilty!" This is a very good legal tradition that originated in England under King Richard III. Just imagine what it would be like to be punished for a crime you did not commit. Almost no one is willing to take another person's punishment. Therefore, it is not surprising that stories of wrongful accusations appear in the literature of England and the United States, countries that cherish the innocent-until-proven-guilty principle.

EXERCISE 7.5: Confirmation and Refutation in Crime Detection

Directions: Please read the introductory note. Then read the excerpt from *The Adventures of Tom Sawyer* by Mark Twain. After reading, answer the questions that follow.

Mark Twain
1835-1910

BACKGROUND: *In this excerpt from* The Adventures of Tom Sawyer *by Mark Twain, Tom Sawyer and his friend Huckleberry Finn have sneaked out at midnight to take a dead cat to a graveyard in a superstitious effort to get rid of warts. Frightened when they hear the voices of three men in the graveyard, they hide behind a tree to observe what happens. The three men turn out to be a young doctor, a man named Muff Potter, and the villain of the story, Injun Joe. At the time the book was written (1876), it was not legal to dissect human bodies for scientific research, so doctors who desired to do such research, had to pay grave robbers to dig up bodies for them to study in secret. This is the reason why the doctor, Muff Potter, and Injun Joe have come to the graveyard at midnight.*

From Chapter IX

Some vague figures approached through the gloom, swinging an old-fashioned tin lantern that freckled the ground with innumerable little spangles of light. Presently Huckleberry whispered with a shudder:

"It's the devils sure enough. Three of 'em! Lordy, Tom, we're goners! Can you pray?"

"I'll try, but don't you be afeard. They ain't going to hurt us. 'Now I lay me down to sleep, I –'

"Sh!"

"What is it, Huck?"

"They're HUMANS! One of 'em is, anyway. One of 'em's old Muff Potter's voice."

"No -- 'tain't so, is it?"

"I bet I know it. Don't you stir nor budge. He ain't sharp enough to notice us. Drunk, the same as usual, likely -- blamed old rip!"

"All right, I'll keep still. Now they're stuck. Can't find it. Here they come again. Now they're hot. Cold again. Hot again. Red hot! They're p'inted right, this time. Say, Huck, I know another o' them voices; it's Injun Joe."

"That's so -- that murderin' half-breed! I'd druther they was devils a dern sight. What kin they be up to?"

The whisper died wholly out now, for the three men had reached the grave and stood within a few feet of the boys' hiding-place.

"Here it is," said the third voice; and the owner of it held the lantern up and revealed the face of young Doctor Robinson.

Potter and Injun Joe were carrying a handbarrow with a rope and a couple of shovels on it. They cast down their load and began to open the grave. The doctor put the lantern at the head of the grave and came and sat down with his back against one of the elm trees. He was so close the boys could have touched him.

"Hurry, men!" he said, in a low voice; "the moon might come out at any moment."

They growled a response and went on digging. For some time there was no noise but the grating sound of the spades discharging their freight of mould and gravel. It was very monotonous. Finally a spade struck upon the coffin with a dull woody accent, and within another minute or two the men had hoisted it out on the ground. They pried off the lid with their shovels, got out the body and dumped it rudely on the ground. The moon drifted from behind the clouds and exposed the pallid face. The barrow was got ready and the corpse placed on it, covered with a blanket, and bound to its place with the rope. Potter took out a large spring-knife and cut off the dangling end of the rope and then said:

"Now the cussed thing's ready, Sawbones, and you'll just out with another five, or here she stays."

"That's the talk!" said Injun Joe.

"Look here, what does this mean?" said the doctor. "You required your pay in advance, and I've paid you."

"Yes, and you done more than that," said Injun Joe, approaching the doctor, who was now standing. "Five years ago you drove me away from your father's kitchen one night, when I come to ask for something to eat, and you said I warn't there for any good; and when I swore I'd get even with you if it took a hundred years, your father had me jailed for a vagrant. Did you think I'd forget? The Injun blood ain't in me for nothing. And now I've GOT you, and you got to SETTLE, you know!"

He was threatening the doctor, with his fist in his face, by this time. The doctor struck out suddenly and stretched the ruffian on the ground. Potter dropped his knife, and exclaimed:

"Here, now, don't you hit my pard!" and the next moment he had grappled with the doctor and the two were struggling with might and main, trampling the grass and tearing the ground with their heels. Injun Joe sprang to his feet, his eyes flaming with passion, snatched up Potter's knife, and went creeping, catlike and stooping, round and round about the combatants, seeking an opportunity. All at once the doctor flung himself free, seized the heavy headboard of Williams' grave and felled Potter to the earth with it -- and in the same instant the half-breed saw his chance and drove the knife to the hilt in the young man's breast. He reeled and fell partly upon Potter, flooding him with his blood, and in the same moment the clouds blotted out the dreadful spectacle and the two frightened boys went speeding away in the dark.

Presently, when the moon emerged again, Injun Joe was standing over the two forms, contemplating them. The doctor murmured inarticulately, gave a long gasp or two and was still. The half-breed muttered:

"THAT score is settled — . . ."

Then he robbed the body. After which he put the fatal knife in Potter's open right hand, and sat down on the dismantled coffin. Three -- four -- five minutes passed, and then Potter began to stir and moan. His hand closed upon the knife; he raised it, glanced at it, and let it fall, with a shudder. Then he sat up, pushing the body from him, and gazed at it, and then around him, confusedly. His eyes met Joe's.

"Lord, how is this, Joe?" he said.

"It's a dirty business," said Joe, without moving.

"What did you do it for?"

"I! I never done it!"

"Look here! That kind of talk won't wash."

Potter trembled and grew white.

"I thought I'd got sober. I'd no business to drink to-night. But it's in my head yet -- worse'n when we started here. I'm all in a muddle; can't recollect anything of it, hardly. Tell me, Joe -- HONEST, now, old feller -- did I do it? Joe, I never meant to -- 'pon my soul and honor, I never meant to, Joe. Tell me how it was, Joe. Oh, it's awful -- and him so young and promising."

"Why, you two was scuffling, and he fetched you one with the headboard and you fell flat; and then up you come, all reeling and staggering like, and snatched the knife and jammed it into him, just as he fetched you another awful clip -- and here you've laid, as dead as a wedge til now."

"Oh, I didn't know what I was a-doing. I wish I may die this minute if I did. It was all on account of the whiskey and the excitement, I reckon. I never used a weepon in my life before, Joe. I've fought, but never with weepons. They'll all say that. Joe, don't tell! Say you won't tell, Joe -- that's a good feller. I always liked you, Joe, and stood up for you, too. Don't you remember? You WON'T tell, WILL you, Joe?" And the poor creature dropped on his knees before the stolid murderer, and clasped his appealing hands.

"No, you've always been fair and square with me, Muff Potter, and I won't go back on you. There, now, that's as fair as a man can say."

"Oh, Joe, you're an angel. I'll bless you for this the longest day I live." And Potter began to cry.

"Come, now, that's enough of that. This ain't any time for blubbering. You be off yonder way and I'll go this. Move, now, and don't leave any tracks behind you."

Potter started on a trot that quickly increased to a run. The half-breed stood looking after him. He muttered:

"If he's as much stunned with the lick and fuddled with the rum as he had the look of being, he won't think of the knife till he's gone so far he'll be afraid to come back after it to such a place by himself -- chicken-heart!"

Two or three minutes later the murdered man, the blanketed corpse, the lidless coffin, and the open grave were under no inspection but the moon's. The stillness was complete again, too.

From CHAPTER XI

Close upon the hour of noon the whole village was suddenly electrified with the ghastly news. No need of the as yet undreamed-of telegraph; the tale flew from man to man, from group to group, from house to house, with little less than telegraphic speed. Of course the schoolmaster gave holiday for that afternoon; the town would have thought strangely of him if he had not.

A gory knife had been found close to the murdered man, and it had been recognized by somebody as belonging to Muff Potter -- so the story ran. And it was said that a belated citizen had come upon Potter washing himself in the "branch" [creek] about one or two o'clock in the morning, and that Potter had at once sneaked off -- suspicious circumstances, especially the washing which was not a habit with Potter. It was also said that the town had been ransacked for this "murderer" (the public are not slow in the matter of sifting evidence and arriving at a verdict), but that he could not be found. Horsemen had departed down all the roads in every direction, and the Sheriff "was confident" that he would be captured before night.

All the town was drifting toward the graveyard. Tom's heartbreak vanished and he joined the procession, not because he would not a thousand times rather go anywhere else, but because an awful, unaccountable fascination drew him on. Arrived at the dreadful place, he wormed his small body through the crowd and saw the dismal spectacle. It seemed to him an age since he was there before. Somebody pinched his arm. He turned, and his eyes met Huckleberry's. Then both looked elsewhere at once, and wondered if anybody had noticed anything in their mutual glance. But everybody was talking, and intent upon the grisly spectacle before them.

"Poor fellow!" "Poor young fellow!" "This ought to be a lesson to grave robbers!" "Muff Potter'll hang for this if they catch him!" This was the drift of remark; and the minister said, "It was a judgment; His hand is here."

Now Tom shivered from head to heel; for his eye fell upon the stolid face of Injun Joe. At this moment the crowd began to sway and struggle, and voices shouted, "It's him! it's him! he's coming himself!"

"Who? Who?" from twenty voices.

"Muff Potter!"

"Hallo, he's stopped! -- Look out, he's turning! Don't let him get away!"

People in the branches of the trees over Tom's head said he wasn't trying to get away -- he only looked doubtful and perplexed.

"Infernal impudence!" said a bystander; "wanted to come and take a quiet look at his work, I reckon -- didn't expect any company."

The crowd fell apart, now, and the Sheriff came through, ostentatiously leading Potter by the arm. The poor fellow's face was haggard, and his eyes showed the fear that was upon him. When he stood before the murdered man, he shook as with a palsy, and he put his face in his hands and burst into tears.

"I didn't do it, friends," he sobbed; "'pon my word and honor I never done it."

"Who's accused you?" shouted a voice.

This shot seemed to carry home. Potter lifted his face and looked around him with a pathetic hopelessness in his eyes. He saw Injun Joe, and exclaimed:

"Oh, Injun Joe, you promised me you'd never --"

"Is that your knife?" and it was thrust before him by the Sheriff.

Potter would have fallen if they had not caught him and eased him to the ground. Then he said:

"Something told me 't if I didn't come back and get --" He shuddered; then waved his nerveless hand with a vanquished gesture and said, "Tell 'em, Joe, tell 'em -- it ain't any use any more."

Then Huckleberry and Tom stood dumb and staring, and heard the stony-hearted liar reel off his serene statement, they expecting every moment that the clear sky would deliver God's lightnings upon his head, and wondering to see how long the stroke was delayed. And when he had finished and still stood alive and whole, their wavering impulse to break their oath and save the poor betrayed prisoner's life faded and vanished away, for plainly this miscreant had sold himself to Satan and it would be fatal to meddle with the property of such a power as that.

"Why didn't you leave? What did you want to come here for?" somebody said.

"I couldn't help it -- I couldn't help it," Potter moaned. "I wanted to run away, but I couldn't seem to come anywhere but here." And he fell to sobbing again. . . .

Questions:

1. The reader knows that Muff Potter did not stab the doctor. However, the villagers seem to think that Muff is guilty. What evidence is there to suggest that it is **possible** Muff Potter stabbed the doctor?

2. What evidence is there to suggest that it is **probable** Muff Potter is guilty?

3. What makes it **clear** that Muff knew about the crime?

4. Is the evidence **consistent** with the conclusion the villagers have reached?

Quills #2

Pretend that you are an attorney who is going to speak in defense of Muff Potter. You have done your homework: (a) you have examined all of the evidence; (b) you have talked to Muff Potter; and (c) you have talked to the witnesses, Tom Sawyer and Huckleberry Finn. Write a speech to persuade the jury that Oliver Twist is innocent of the charge of theft. Use the approaches we have studied in this chapter: Impossible, Improbable, Unclear, and Inconsistent. Follow this organization pattern: Narrative, Opinion, Approaches, Conclusion.

COMMONPLACE

Chapter 8

Introduction

In Exodus 19-20, we read the narrative about how God gave the Ten Commandments to Moses on Mount Sinai. They were as follows:

The Ten Commandments
From Exodus 20

>You shall have no other gods before me.
>
>You shall not make for yourself a carved image. . . . You shall not bow down to them or serve them.
>
>You shall not take the name of the LORD your God in vain. . . .
>
>Remember the Sabbath day, to keep it holy. . . .
>
>Honor your father and your mother. . . .
>
>You shall not murder.
>
>You shall not commit adultery.
>
>You shall not steal.
>
>You shall not bear false witness against your neighbor.
>
>You shall not covet. . . .

Now, the Commandments seem fairly clear, but people usually have a lot of questions anyway. Take, for example, the ninth commandment: "You shall not bear false witness against your neighbor." People often ask questions like these:

1. What exactly does it mean to "bear false witness"?
2. Can you give an example?
3. Is lying to protect someone's feelings the same as bearing false witness?
4. What is the opposite of bearing false witness?
5. What might cause someone to bear false witness?
6. What bad results might happen when someone bears false witness?
7. Should we punish a person who bears false witness?

Now, the Ten Commandments help us know what is good behavior and what is bad behavior. But when we go into the details, answering all the questions we might have about a behavior, we are creating what the Greeks called a Commonplace.

In this chapter, you will learn the various approaches to writing about a behavior—either good or bad. You will also have the opportunity to practice writing a Commonplace.

Definition and Purpose

1. A Commonplace is a composition about a vice, that is, a bad behavior. Whenever we study human beings, we are reminded that, as the apostle Paul put it, "For all have sinned and fall short of the glory of God" (Romans 3:23). This passage tells us there are probably a lot of behaviors to write about!

2. Teachers in ancient times said that the purpose of the Commonplace was to teach people to shun vice and to develop virtue. But what exactly is a vice or a virtue? Fortunately, for us, we can look to the Bible to guide us in this matter.

Approaches to the Commonplace

Below is a chart that explains the five approaches to the Commonplace:

Contrast	Make a statement about the opposite of the virtue or vice. • For example, if you are writing about the vice of lying, you would state that the opposite of lying is truthfulness.
Comparison	Compare the vice to something that is similar but even worse. • For example, the disobedience of a child is similar to man's disobedience to God.
Cause X ⟶ Y	Explain why someone might actually commit a sin. • For example, people might think that telling a lie would help them to avoid punishment or to get things they want.
Example e.g.	Offer an example of the vice you are describing. • For example, you might narrate an event from history, from the Bible, or from a great work of literature (such as *Pinocchio*).
Call for Punishment	Explain why the vice should be punished. • For example, you could describe the ill effect the vice has had on others—or even on the persons who commit the vice.

Organization

The best organization plan is as follows:

1. Write a general statement about the vice you will discuss.
2. Clearly state your position about the vice.
3. Write one well-developed paragraph to explain each approach in the chart above.
4. Write a short conclusion that summarizes your main points.

Model Commonplace

Against School Bullying

General Statement

Playground and classroom bullying have become a big problem in schools across the United States in recent years. Bullying is not limited to hitting or kicking. It also includes name calling, gossip, and actions like excluding people from the group or setting up situations that will cause someone to be embarrassed.

Writer's Position

Parents, teachers, and students must take a stand against bullying.

Contrast

The opposite of bullying is showing kindness and friendship. Bullies think of themselves first. Friends consider the feelings of others.

Comparison

Bullying is similar to the behavior of tyrants. Tyrants like Germany's Adolf Hitler, Russia's Joseph Stalin, Italy's Benito Mussolini, Uganda's Idi Amin, and Cambodia's Pol Pot were

Benito Mussolini
1883-1945

nothing more than overgrown playground bullies who graduated from the playground to their nations' capital cities. They were very willing to imprison, hurt, and even kill people who did not agree with them.

Example

Bullying on the Internet is called cyber-bullying. One example of cyber-bullying involved a girl named Catherine whose classmates began saying mean things to her on Facebook. Then a few weeks later they actually attacked her at a party and even broke some of the bones in her face.[35]

Call for Punishment

In schools across the United States, there are several kinds of punishment for bullying. Students might be suspended, expelled, required to pay fines, or even serve jail time. Also, some states charge huge fines to school districts which do not get control of bullying.[36]

Conclusion

In short, bullying is a sinful behavior that families, schools, and communities need to oppose and punish in order for people to live happily together.

EXERCISE 8.1: Analyzing a Commonplace

<u>Directions</u>: Analyze "Against School Bullying" by answering the following questions.

1. In the General Statement, the writer begins with a statement against school bullying. What seems to be the purpose of the other two sentences in the paragraph?

2. In Writer's Position, begin with the helping verb *must* and write the five words that show the writer's position.

   . . . must _____ _____ _____ _____ _____.

3. In Contrast, the writer contrasts bullying with showing _____ and

   _____.

4. In Comparison, the writer compares bullies with _____.

5. Which of the following best describes the writer's Example?

   A. It is about a case of physical violence.

   B. It is about a case of cyber-bullying.

   C. It is about a case of cyber-bullying that turned into physical violence.

6. Underline the five punishments that are listed in Call for Punishment.

EXERCISE 8.2: Brainstorming Contrast and Comparison

Directions: With a partner or with the class-at-large, brainstorm some ideas for Commonplace compositions. At the left, you will see a vice. In the other two columns, suggest behaviors that would serve as contrasts and comparisons. The first one serves as an example.

Vice	Contrast (Opposite Behavior)	Comparison (Similar Behavior)
Disobedience to Parents	*Obedience to parents*	*Disobedience to the law*
Never Returning What Was Borrowed		
Throwing Tantrums to Get One's Way		
Being a Picky Eater		

EXERCISE 8.3: Brainstorming Examples

 With a partner or with the class-at-large, brainstorm examples for the following vices. Your example can be from real life or from a book you have read. The first one serves as an example.

Vice	Example
Disobedience	*Pinocchio's disobedience to Gepetto*
Cheating in a Game	
Carelessness with Property	
Using Bad Language	

Quills: Commonplace

 Your teacher will give you the instructions you need to write a Commonplace.

COMPARISON

Chapter 9

Introduction

Most of us know the story from Grimm's fairy tales called "Cinderella," which is about a sweet girl whose mother dies, leaving her with her dear father. The father takes a second wife, and then things change for his daughter. The author tells it this way:

The woman had brought two daughters into the house with her, who were beautiful and fair of face, but vile and black of heart. Now began a bad time for the poor step-child. "Is the stupid goose to sit in the parlour with us?" said they. "He who wants to eat bread must earn it; out with the kitchen-wench." They took her pretty clothes away from her, put an old grey bed gown on her, and gave her wooden shoes. "Just look at the proud princess, how decked out she is!" they cried, and laughed, and led her into the kitchen. There she had to do hard work from morning till night, get up before daybreak, carry water, light fires, cook and wash. Besides this, the sisters did her every imaginable injury—they mocked her and emptied her peas and lentils into the ashes, so that she was forced to sit and pick them out again. In the evening when she had worked till she was weary she had no bed to go to, but had to sleep by the fireside in the ashes. And as on that account she always looked dusty and dirty, they called her Cinderella. It happened that the father was once going to the fair, and he asked his two step-daughters what he should bring back for them. "Beautiful dresses," said one,

"Pearls and jewels," said the second. "And thou, Cinderella," said he, "what wilt thou have?" "Father, break off for me the first branch which knocks against your hat on your way home."[37]

Now, at the base of this story is a writing technique called Comparison. Cinderella's original life and the life she had as a step-daughter are very different.

 **THINK IT THROUGH:**

- With your classmates, make a list the differences, which the reader can perceive in this passage from "Cinderella." (HINT: You should be able to find five.)

- If we compared Cinderella and her step-sisters, what character traits would we praise in Cinderella and blame in the step-sisters?

As you can see in these excerpts from "Cinderella," it is possible to use Comparison not only for simple description, but also to teach something about vice and virtue.

The purpose of this chapter is to introduce the progymnasmata element Comparison and give you an opportunity to practice it.

Definition and Purpose of Comparison

1. A Comparison is an essay or speech that lists and discusses similarities and/or differences between such things as the following:

   - Two people

   - Two things

   - Two occasions (such as holidays)

   - Two activities (such as sports)

   - Two animals (species or individual animals)

- Two plants

- Two stories or characters in stories

2. The Greek teacher Aphthonius showed that Comparison is related to Encomium and Invective because we often praise or blame the things we compare. We see this element at work in the story of Cinderella. Cinderella is the object of Encomium while the stepsisters are the object of Invective.

3. In our own times, textbook writers often compare two things in order to instruct the readers. For example, the science textbook might compare different kinds of clouds. In this case, praise or blame is not normally used.

THINK IT THROUGH:

- In music class, what two musical instruments could you compare?

- In geography, what two rivers could you compare?

- In science class, what two trees could you compare?

EXERCISE 9.1: Analyzing a Biblical Comparison

Directions: In his earthly ministry, Jesus often used comparisons to make a point. For an example, please examine the Scripture passage below. Then answer the questions that follow.

The Narrow Gate
Matthew 7:13-14

"[13] Enter by the narrow gate. For the gate is wide and the way is easy that leads to destruction, and those who enter by it are many. [14] For the gate is narrow and the way is hard that leads to life, and those who find it are few."

Christian Enters the Wicket Gate in *Pilgrim's Progress*

1. Like many of Jesus' comparisons, Matthew 7:13-14 contains a double comparison. For starters, examine the two gates that are described by comparing the elements of the gates. The first one serves as an example.

Element	Gate of Verse 13	Gate of Verse 14
Size	wide	narrow
Way (Road)		
What It Leads To		
How Many Enter		

2. In the first sentence of the passage, which of the gates does Jesus tell us to enter?

3. Considering both verses, which of the following seems to best sum up why heading for the narrow gate is the better choice?

   A. It is not so difficult a journey.

   B. The destination is better.

   C. There are more friends to make the trip more enjoyable.

4. Now let us consider the second comparison, the comparison of the roads to ways of life and the gates to the after-life.

   a. Verse 13 describes the road and the gate to _____.

   b. Verse 14 describes the road and the gate to _____.

EXERCISE 9.2: Practicing Transitions of Similarity

Directions: In the exercise below, you will see two sentences in each problem. On a piece of notebook paper, write out the sentences and join them with the transition indicated in the parentheses. Be sure to use a comma after each transition. When finished, underline the transition. The first one will serve as an example.

1. (Use *similarly*.)
   Bacon and eggs are served at breakfast.
   Ham and cheese are served at lunch.

   Bacon and eggs are served at breakfast. Similarly, ham and cheese are served at lunch.

2. (Use *likewise*.)
   Cotton candy is often enjoyed at the circus.
   Popcorn is often enjoyed at a movie.

3. (Use *in much the same way.*)

In Charades, the team must guess what a player is acting out.

In Pictionary, the team must guess what a player has sketched.

4. (Use *however.*)

The Jamestown settlement was mostly made up of men.

Plymouth Plantation was mostly made up of families.

5. (Use *in contrast.*)

The Sioux *tipi* was made of buffalo skins.

The Wampanoag *wetu* was made of sticks and grass.

SIOUX TIPI

WAMPANOAG WETU

Model Comparison

Differences between Jamestown and Plymouth Plantation

(1) The Jamestown Settlement of Virginia and the Plymouth Plantation in what became Massachusetts were different in several ways. (2) First, the two settlements were started for different reasons. (3) Jamestown was founded primarily to expand trade for the English. (4) On the other hand, Plymouth was founded for the religious freedom of the Puritans who had decided to leave the Church of England (that is, the Separatists). (5) Second, the background of the two groups of settlers was

different. (6) The inhabitants of Jamestown were mainly aristocratic gentlemen who knew nothing of agriculture and were not accustomed to difficult labor. (7) However, the founders of Plymouth were yeomen and tradesmen with their wives and children, people who were willing to work hard to produce crops and survive in the wilderness. (8) Last, the relations between each group and the Natives were different. (9) The Jamestown settlers at first engaged in welcome trade with the Indians, but since the English depended heavily on the Indians to supply their food, tension mounted and violence sometimes occurred. (10) In contrast, at Plymouth, through the assistance of the Indian known as Squanto, the settlers learned how to farm in the New World and relations between the settlers and the Wampanoag of the area were good for forty years.

EXERCISE 9.3: Analyzing the Model Comparison

Directions: Analyze the paragraph about the Jamestown Settlement and Plymouth Plantation by answering the following questions.

1. Begin by creating the zigzag scheme for this paragraph on the chalkboard.

2. Look at Sentence 1, the topic sentence. The general topic is the English settlements in Jamestown and Plymouth Plantation. What is the controlling idea?

3. What are the listing transitions that lead the reader from point to point?

   Sentence 2: _____

   Sentence 5: _____

   Sentence 8: _____

4. What transitions are used to contrast the two settlements?

   Sentence 4: _____

   Sentence 7: _____

   Sentence 10: _____

5. What are the three differences named in Sentences 2, 5, and 8?

   Sentence 2: _____

   Sentence 5: _____

   Sentence 8: _____

Model Comparison with Encomium and Invective

Differences between Tsar Alexander II and Tsar Alexander III

(1) Tsar Alexander II of Russia was much more democratic than his son, Tsar Alexander III in several ways. (2) First, Alexander II, the father, started education for the children of the poor. (3) However, Alexander III forced schools to raise their tuition so that fewer poor children could attend. (4) Second, Alexander II reformed the legal system. (5) He made it possible for local communities to elect their own judges and introduced trial by jury, which reduced the power of the rich. (6) Alexander III, on the other hand, placed restrictions on jurors. (7) He again showed favoritism to the rich by making sure that only the wealthier people could serve on juries. (8) Third, Alexander II was tolerant of the press. (9) He did not become upset when writers criticized the government. (10) In contrast, Alexander III banned publications that did not support his policies. (11) In short, Alexander III was much less democratic than his father, Tsar Alexander II.

Alexander II
1818-1821

Alexander III
1845-1894

EXERCISE 9.4: Analyzing the Model Comparison

<u>Directions</u>: Analyze the paragraph about Tsars Alexander III and Alexander II by answering the following questions.

1. Begin by creating the zigzag scheme for this paragraph on the chalkboard.

Student Text

2. Look at Sentence 1, the topic sentence. What part of the controlling idea suggests this comparison will use praise (Encomium) and blame (Invective)?

3. What are the listing transitions that lead the reader from point to point?

   Sentence 2: _____

   Sentence 4: _____

   Sentence 8: _____

4. What transitions are used to contrast the two tsars?

   Sentence 3: _____

   Sentence 6: _____

   Sentence 10: _____

5. What are the three differences named in Sentences 2, 4, and 8?

   Sentence 2: _____

   Sentence 4: _____

   Sentence 8: _____

6. Is Invective directed toward Alexander II or Alexander III in this paragraph?

7. What words are used to suggest Invective?

   Sentence 3: _____

   Sentence 7: _____

   Sentence 10: _____

Quills: Comparison

 Your teacher will give you the instructions you need to write a Comparison..

SPEECH-IN-CHARACTER

Chapter 10

Introduction

Below is an excerpt from a poem by Rudyard Kipling (1865-1936). Kipling was born to English parents living in Bombay, India, during the time of the British Empire. As a young man, he was associate editor for a newspaper in Lahore and covered the story of a meeting between the British Viceroy in India and the Amir of Afghanistan, whom the British hoped to impress. Kipling later wrote a story based on this event entitled "Her Majesty's Service," in which two soldiers go out at night and listen to the military animals "talking." The poem "Parade Song of the Camp Animals" is included at the end of the story. The excerpt below is Kipling's depiction of what a military camel might have said, if he could have spoken.

Commissariat Camels
By Rudyard Kipling

We haven't a camelty tune of our own
To help us trollop along,
But every neck is a hair-trombone
(Rtt-ta-ta-ta! is a hair-trombone!)
And this is our marching-song:
Can't! Don't! Shan't! Won't!
Pass it along the line!

Somebody's pack has slid from his back,
'Wish it were only mine!
Somebody's load has tipped off in the road—
Cheer for a halt and a row!
Urrr! Yarrh! Grr! Arrh!
Somebody's catching it now![38]

 **THINK IT THROUGH:**

- What features of the poem suggest that a camel is speaking?
- What attitude does the camel display towards his job?

This short poem illustrates an element of the progymnasmata called Speech-in-Character, which you will learn about and practice in this chapter.

Definition and Purpose of Speech-in-Character

1. A Speech-in-Character is the speech of a character in a poem, play, story, or novel.

2. Its purpose is to reveal something about the personality of the speaker, especially when placed in a difficult situation.

3. It is written in such a way that the word choice reflects the nature of the speaker. A soldier might not speak the same way as a dairy maid, for example.

Content of a Speech-in-Character

When you write a Speech-in-Character, you will begin by creating a character and putting him or her into some kind of situation. Some examples are the following:

- I'm in a bad situation. What got me into it? What can I do about it?

- I'm in a bad situation. What got me into it? What could make it even worse?

- I'm in a good situation. How is it better than my past situation? Can I maintain it?

- I'm in a good situation. Here's how it came about. What could make it even better?

Notice that in these examples, all three of the time periods are involved: past, present, and future. This means that verb tense will be a factor in the composition. You will learn more about that below.

As its name Speech-in-Character indicates, this type of composition depends on the creation of a character. It might be helpful to recall the topics for describing people from Chapter 2:

- Name

- Age

- Gender

- Nationality/Ethnic Group

- Appearance

- Mental/Emotional Condition

All of these are important when writing a Speech-in-Character because all these elements will influence how the character feels about and approaches his or her situation: past, present, and future.

- A young character might be filled with hope, for example. An older one might realize that death is approaching.

- One person might feel helpless in the same situation that would make another ready to fight.

It will be important for you to put yourself into your character's shoes, so to speak, to understand and communicate what he or she feels.

EXERCISE 10.1: Thinking about Character

Directions: Below are some more excerpts from Kipling's poem "Parade Song of the Camp Animals." Each animal has its own characteristic way of speaking. The questions below will help you to see what Kipling did to reveal each animal's personality and attitude.

A. Cavalry Horses

By the brand on my withers, the finest of tunes
Is played by the Lancers, Hussars, and Dragoons,
And it's sweeter than "Stables" or "Water" to me,
The Cavalry Canter of "Bonnie Dundee!"
Then feed us and break us and handle and groom,
And give us good riders and plenty of room,
The Way of the War-horse to "Bonnie Dundee!"[39]

1. In every line, Kipling uses a beat like this:

    ta-ta-TA / ta-ta-TA / ta-ta-TA / ta-ta-TA

    Why is this sound a particularly good one to represent cavalry horses?

2. Unlike the camel, the horse is not complaining. What words would you use to describe the horse's attitude toward his assignment?

B. Screw-Gun Mules

As me and my companions were scrambling up a hill,
The path was lost in rolling stones, but we went forward still;
For we can wriggle and climb, my lads, an turn up everywhere
And it's our delight on a mountain height, with a leg or two to spare!

Good luck to every sergeant, then, that lets us pick our road:
Bad luck to all the driver-men that cannot pack a load!

For we can wriggle and climb, my lads, and turn up everywhere,
And it's our delight on a mountain height, with a leg or two to spare!

3. On the opening line, the mule has a grammar mistake. What is it, and why do you suppose Kipling gave this type of mistake to a mule?

4. Which characteristic of mules, in general, makes this particular mule proud?

5. The mule does not stride beautifully like a war horse. How does the mule unashamedly describe the movement of his species?

C. Elephants of the Gun Teams

> We lent to Alexander the strength of Hercules,
> The wisdom of our foreheads, the cunning of our knees.
> We bowed our necks to service—they ne'er were loosed again,—
> Make way there, way for the ten-foot teams
> Of the Forty-Pounder train!

6. In the first two lines, the elephant seems almost to be bragging. How far back in time does he note that the service of military elephants goes?

7. Why do you suppose he mentions Alexander and Hercules, in particular?

8. Why do you suppose Kipling has the elephant say, "Make way there, way for the ten-foot teams / Of the Forty-Pounder train!"?

9. The animals in "Parade Song of the Camp Animals" use various time frames in their poems. For example the elephant talks about history in past tense. What tense is the command, "Make way there"?

Verb Tense Options in a Speech-in-Character

The elephant of the gun team used past to talk about the elephant's role in ancient wars and present tense (in a command) to refer to his present situation. The command ("Make way there") also hints about what is going to happen next. He's going forward for a reason.

This use of more than one verb tense is not unusual for a Speech-in-Character. In fact, some speeches of this type occur in stories where characters find themselves in some kind of predicament. They stop to think things over, and we listen as they describe their problem, review how they got into the problem, and try to figure out how to get out of the problem.

Model Speech-in-Character

Below is an excerpt from the novel *Peter Pan* (1911) by J. M. Barrie (1860-1937), where Captain Hook cooks up a plot by which he can catch the Lost Boys, who he knows are hiding in an underground room. After reading the excerpt, answer the questions in "Think It Through."

Excerpt from *Peter Pan*
By J. M. Barrie

"Did you hear them say Peter Pan's from home?" Smee whispered, fidgeting with Johnny Corkscrew.

Hook nodded. He stood for a long time lost in thought, and at last a curdling smile lit up his swarthy face. Smee had been waiting for it. "Unrip your plan, captain," he cried eagerly.

"To return to the ship," Hook replied slowly through his teeth, "and cook a large rich cake of a jolly thickness with green sugar on it. There can be but one room below, for there is but one chimney. The silly moles had not the sense to see that they did not need a door apiece. That shows they have no mother. We will leave the cake on the shore of the Mermaids' Lagoon. These boys are always swimming about there, playing with the mermaids. They will find the cake and they will gobble it up, because, having no mother, they don't know how dangerous 'tis to eat rich damp cake." He burst into laughter, not hollow laughter now, but honest laughter. "Aha, they will die."[40]

ROB HARWOOD PORTRAYING CAPTAIN HOOK, 1906

THINK IT THROUGH:

- **Past tense:** What mistake did the boys make when they went underground?
- **Present tense:** What does this mistake indicate to Hook about the boys' situation?
- **Future tense:** What does Hook plan to do to catch them?

Organizing a Speech-in-Character

One way to write a Speech-in-Character is to use this formula:

Present + Past + Future.

1. **Present:** Here's my predicament.
2. **Past:** Here's how I got into my predicament.
3. **Future:** Here's what may happen next because of my predicament.

OR

Here's what I'm going to do to get out of my predicament.

EXERCISE 10.2: Analysis of Speech-in-Character

<u>Directions</u>: Please begin by reading the introductory note. Then read the excerpt and answer the questions that follow.

Charles Dickens
1812-1870

NOTE: The excerpt below comes from the last chapter in A Christmas Carol *(1843) by the British author Charles Dickens (1812-70). Ebenezer Scrooge is a stingy, grumpy man who begrudges giving his employee Bob Cratchitt a day off to celebrate Christmas with his family, which includes a little crippled boy named Tiny Tim. Scrooge has no happiness in life and, regarding Christmas, has nothing to say but, "Bah! Humbug!" On Christmas Eve, he is visited by three spirits: the Ghost of Christmas Past (who shows him the time when he was too busy with his job to marry the girl who loved him); the Ghost of Christmas Present (who shows him his nephew's Christmas party, where the nephew's wife call him stingy); and the Ghost of Christmas Future (who shows him the scene of his death when the cleaning lady is happily stealing the curtains from his four-poster bed.) Then he suddenly awakes and—glad to be alive—resoundingly speaks about his experience.*

[1] "They are not torn down," cried Scrooge, folding one of his bed-curtains in his arms, "they are not torn down, rings and all. They are here—I am here—the shadows of the things that would have been, may be dispelled. They will be. I know they will!" . . .

[2] "I don't know what to do!" cried Scrooge, laughing and crying in the same breath; and making a perfect Laocoön of himself with his stockings. "I am as light as a feather, I am as happy as an angel, I am as merry as a schoolboy. I am as giddy as a drunken man. A merry Christmas to everybody! A happy New Year to all the world. Hallo here! Whoop! Hallo!" . . .

[3] "There's the saucepan that the gruel was in!" cried Scrooge, starting off again, and going round the fireplace. "There's the door, by which the Ghost of Jacob Marley entered! There's the corner where the Ghost of Christmas Present sat! There's the window where I saw the wandering Spirits! It's all right, it's all true, it all happened. Ha ha ha!" . . .

[4] "I don't know what day of the month it is!" said Scrooge. "I don't know how long I've been among the Spirits. I don't know anything. I'm quite a baby. Never mind. I don't care. I'd rather be a baby. Hallo! Whoop! Hallo here!" *[He calls to a boy in the street and asks him to buy*

the biggest turkey at the poultry shop and bring it to him. He then has it sent to Bob Cratchit's family, whom he visits to wish the family Merry Christmas.]

[5] "A merry Christmas, Bob!" said Scrooge, with an earnestness that could not be mistaken, as he clapped him on the back. "A merrier Christmas, Bob, my good fellow, than I have given you, for many a year! I'll raise your salary, and endeavour to assist your struggling family, and we will discuss your affairs this very afternoon, over a Christmas bowl of smoking bishop, Bob! Make up the fires, and buy another coal-scuttle before you dot another *i*, Bob Cratchit!"

Questions:

1. In Paragraphs 1-2, Scrooge speaks in present tense, describing what he sees and expressing his emotion.

    a. What does he see?

    b. Why does this cause him to feel so happy?

2. In Paragraph 3, Scrooge speaks in past tense. What is he seeing and thinking about here?

3. Paragraph 4 brings Scrooge back to the present time. Then in Paragraph 5, he visits the family of his employee, Bob Cratchitt. Here Scrooge speaks in future tense. What does he promise to do in the future?

4. What mood has the author created for the reader in this scene?

Quills: Speech-in-Character

 The teacher will give you the instructions you need to show your ability to write a Speech-in-Character. Remember to let the character's personality and emotions show up in his or her speech.

Endnotes

1 George A. Kennedy, *Progymnasmata: Greek Textbooks of Prose Composition and Rhetoric*. Atlanta: Society of Biblical Literature, 2003. xi–xii.
2 Quintilian. *Institutes of Oratory*. Ed. Lee Honeycutt. Trans. John Selby Watson. Iowa State. 2006. Kindle file.
3 Aesop, "The Shepherd's Boy and the Wolf." *Aesop's Fables,* trans. George Fyler Townsend. Chicago: Belford, 1887. 1867. Kindle file.
4 Aesop, "The Lion's Share." Aesop's Fables.
5 Aesop. "The Fly and the Bald Man." *Aesop's Fables*.
6 Aesop. "The Boy Bathing." *Aesop's Fables*. [Slightly edited.]
7 "Washington during the War." *Macmillan's Magazine*. 1862. 6:24. Web. 2 Sept. 2014.
8 "Speech of Frederick Douglass at the Third Decade Celebration of the Anti-Slavery Society in Philadelphia." *Pacific Appeal* [San Francisco]. 31 Feb. 1864. 1. *California Digital Newspaper Collection*. Web. 2 Sept. 2014.
9 The text is a paraphrase of Suetonius' description in "The Personal Traits of Julius Caesar." *Readings in Ancient History: Rome and the West*. Ed. William Stearns Davis. 2:159. Boston: Allyn, 1913.
10 Mark Twain. *The Adventures of Tom Sawyer. 39. Kindle file.*
11 Plutarch. "The Life of Theseus." *Plutarch's Lives*. Vol. 1. Trans. Aubrey Stewart and George Long. London: Bell, 1894. Para. IX. Kindle file.
12 Plutarch. Para. XXXVI.
13 Plutarch. "The Life of Perikles." Para. XXVI.
14 Plutarch. "The Life of Themistokles." Para. XXI.
15 All lines in this exercise are from Robert Louis Stevenson's *A Child's Garden of Voices*. New York: Donohue, 1916.
16 "Teazer the Dog." *Davy Crockett Almanack*. 1847. *Comic Book Plus*. 2014. Web. 12 Sept. 2014.
17 Charles E. Brown. "Paul Bunyan," *Paul Bunyan Tales*. 2nd ed. Madison: U of Wisconsin P, 1927. p. 3. *Hathi Trust*. 14 Mar. 2012. Web. 20 Aug. 2014. <www.hathitrust.org>
18 The examples in this section are taken from *Davy Crockett's Riproarious Shemales and Sentimental Sisters: Women's Tall Tales from the Crockett Almanacs (1835-1856)*. Ed. Michael A. Lofaro. Mechanicsburg, PA: Stackpole, 2001.
19 Davy Crockett. "Fishing in the Atlantic." *Crockett's Almanac 1846*. New York: Turner and Fisher, 1846. Reprint ed. Charleston: Nabu, 2011.
20 Rupert S. Holland. *Historic Boyhoods*. Philadelphia: Jacobs, 1909. Kindle file.
21 Mason Locke Weems. *A History of the Life and Death, Virtues and Exploits of General George Washington*. Philadelphia: Lippincott, 1918. n.p. *We Do American Studies*. University of Virginia. Web. 2 June 2015.
22 "Anecdote." Merriam-Webster.com. n.d. Web. 2 June 2015.
23 Alexander Garden. *Anecdotes of the Revolutionary War*. Charleston: A. E. Miller, 1822. 83-84. Kindle file.
24 "Begging." *The Book of Three Hundred Anecdotes: Historical, Literary, and Humorous*. London: Burnes & Oates, n.d. Kindle file.
25 John Smith. *The General History of Virginia*. Electronic edition. University of North Carolina. 2006. Web. 6 January 2015.
26 Robert Louis Stevenson. *Travels with a Donkey in the Cévannes*. London: Chatto, 1988. 69. Print.
27 Stevenson, 100.
28 William J. Canby. "The History of the Flag of the United States." Transcribed by John B. Harker. *U.S.History.org*. Aug. 1999. Web. 29 Jan. 2015. <http://www.ushistory.org/betsy/more/canby.htm>. Slightly edited for today's punctuation conventions.
29 Hodder, Edwin. *The Life and Work of the Seventh Earl of Shaftesbury, K.G*. London: Cassel, 1886. 2.422. Print.
30 George Richard Jesse. *Researches into the History of the British Dog from Ancient Laws, Charters, and Historical Records*. London: Hardwicke, 1866. Reprint. London: Forgotten Books, 2013. 1.1. Print.
31 William Bradford. *Bradford's History of Plymouth Plantation, 1606-1646*. Ed. William T. Davis. New York: Scribner's, 1908. Kindle file.
32 Charles F. Richardson. *American Literature: 1607-1885*. New York: Putnam's, 1902. 75. HathiTrust.org. n.d. Web. 2 Feb. 2015. <http://catalog.hathitrust.org/Record/001440625>
33 Justin Barr. "Benedict Arnold: Triumph and Treason." *Clio's Eye*. Stephen F. Austin State University. Mar. 2012. Web. 27 Jan 2015.
34 Paul Franklin Baum. "Riddle 42." *Anglo-Saxon Riddles of the* Exeter Book. Durham: Duke UP, 1963. *Wikisource*. 21 Aug 2014. Web. 19 Nov. 2014. Creative Commons Attribution-ShareAlike License. <http://creativecommons.org/licenses/by-sa/3.0/>
35 "Three Real Life Cyber Bullying Stories." *NoBullying.com*. n.d. Web. 28 Oct 2014. <http://nobullying.com/three-real-life-stories-of-cyber-bullying>.
36 "Bullying." *FindLaw*. n.d. Web. 28 Oct 2014. <http://education.findlaw.com/student-conduct-and-discipline/bullying.html>.
37 Brothers Grimm. "Cinderella." Trans. Margaret Hunt, *Grimm's Household Tales*, Vol. 1, 1884. *Wikisource*. Creative Commons Attribution-ShareAlike License. <http://creativecommons.org/licenses/by-sa/3.0/>14 May 2014. Web. 22 Apr. 2015.
38 Rudyard Kipling. "Parade Song of the Animals." *The Jungle Book*. Public Domain. Kindle file.
39 Rudyard Kipling. "Her Majesty's Service." *The Jungle Book*. Public Domain. Kindle file.
40 J. M. Barrie. *Peter and Wendy*. New York: Scribner's, 1911. Public Domain. Kindle file.

Student Text

Image Attribution

Chapter 1, Fable

"The Boy Who Cried Wolf." Francis Barlow. Public Domain. *Wikimedia Commons.* 5 Mar. 2011. Web. 27 May 2015. <http://commons.wikimedia.org/wiki/File:Boycriedwolfbarlow.jpg>.

"The Lion's Share." Francis Barlow. Public Domain. *Wikimedia Commons.* 16 Nov. 2010. Web. 27 May 2015. <http://commons.wikimedia.org/wiki/File:Lion%27s_Share_Barlow.JPG>.

"The Bald Man and the Fly." Wenceslas Hollar. Public Domain. *Wikimedia Commons.* 15 Mar. 2009. Web. 27 May 2015. <http://commons.wikimedia.org/wiki/File:Wenceslas_Hollar_-_The_bald_man_and_the_fly_(State_2).jpg>.

"Good Shepherd." San Calisto Catacomb. Public Domain. *Wikimedia Commons.* 2 Dec. 2011. Web. 27 May 2015. <http://commons.wikimedia.org/wiki/File:Good_shepherd_02b_close.jpg>.

"The Tortoise and the Hare." Arthur Rackham. Public Domain. *Wikimedia Commons.* 15 Apr. 2010. Web. 27 May 2015. <http://commons.wikimedia.org/wiki/File:Tortoise_and_hare_rackham.jpg>.

"La Poule aux Oeufs d'Or." Gustave Doré. Jean de La Fontaine's Fables. Public Domain. *Wikimedia Commons.* 25 Feb. 2008. Web. 27 May 2015. <http://commons.wikimedia.org/wiki/File:La_Poule_aux_Oeufs_d%27Or.jpg>.

Chapter 2, Narrative

Moses bas-relief in the U.S. House of Representatives chamber. Public Domain, *Wikimedia Commons.* 10 Nov. 2006. Web. 27 May 2015. <http://commons.wikimedia.org/wiki/File:Moses_bas-relief_in_the_U.S._House_of_Representatives_chamber.jpg>.

"Theseus and the Minotaur." H. A. Guerber. *The Story of the Greeks.* 1896. PD-US. *Wikimedia Commons.* 21 Apr. 2015. Web. 28 May 2015. <http://commons.wikimedia.org/wiki/File:Theseus_and_the_Minotaur.gif>.

"1839 Crockett Almanac." William Croome. Public Domain. *Wikimedia Commons.* 14 June 2010. Web. 28 May 2015. <http://commons.wikimedia.org/wiki/File:1839_CrockettAlmanac_byWCroome_cover.png>.

"The Paul Bunyan Statue in Portland's Kenton Commercial Historic District." Creative Commons Attribution-Share Alike License 3.0. <http://creativecommons.org/licenses/by-sa/3.0/deed.en>. *Wikimedia Commons.* 1 Feb. 2014. Web. 2 June 2015. <http://commons.wikimedia.org/wiki/File:Paul_Bunyan_Statue_(Kenton_Commercial_Historic_District)-1.jpg>.

"A Battle of the French-Indian War." By Unknown. <http://www.americanrevolution.com/FrenchandIndianWar.htm>. Licensed under Public Domain via *Wikimedia Commons.* <http://commons.wikimedia.org/wiki/File:A_Battle_of_the_French-Indian_War.jpg#/media/File:A_Battle_of_the_French-Indian_War.jpg>.

"Daniel Boone Bicentennial Half Dollar Commemorative Reverse." Public Domain. *Wikimedia Commons.* 28 Mar. 2006. Web. 28 May 2015. <http://commons.wikimedia.org/wiki/File:Daniel_boone_bicentennial_half_dollar_commemorative_reverse.jpg>.

"Boone at Cumberland Gap." Courtesy of U.S. Capitol Historical Society. 2 July 2013. Web. 28 May 2015. <http://www.uschs.org/news-releases/2013-august-brown-bag-lecture-series/>.

"Ethan Allen." The Architect of the Capitol [Larkin G. Mead]. <http://www.aoc.gov/cc/art/nsh/allen_e.cfm.> Licensed under Public Domain via *Wikimedia Commons.* <http://commons.wikimedia.org/wiki/File:Allen_e.jpg#/media/File:Allen_e.jpg>.

"Fort Ticonderoga 1775." Heppenheimer & Maurer. The New York Public Library digital library. Image ID: 808517. Licensed under Public Domain via *Wikimedia Commons.* <http://commons.wikimedia.org/wiki/File:Fort_Ticonderoga_1775.jpg#/media/File:Fort_Ticonderoga_1775.jpg>.

Chapter 3, Description

"Julius Caesar." Chausse Classes. Creative Commons Attribution Share-Alike License 3.0. <http://creativecommons.org/licenses/by-sa/3.0/>. *Wikispaces.* n.d. Web. 28 May 2015. <http://chausseclasses.wikispaces.com/The+Tragedy+of+Julius+Caesar-+Resources>.

"Huckleberry Finn." E. W. Kemble. 1898. PD-US. *Wikimedia Commons.* 19 Sept. 2013. Web. 28 May 2015. <http://commons.wikimedia.org/wiki/File:Huckleberry-finn-with-rabbit.jpg>.

"Irish Need Not Apply." Immigration Museum. *Wikispaces.* n.d. Web. 28 May 2015. <http://immigrationmuseum.wikispaces.com/3.+Irish+Immigrants>.

"Theseus and the Crommyonian Sow." Public Domain. *Wikimedia Commons.* 22 July 2007. Web. 28 May 2015. <http://commons.wikimedia.org/wiki/File:Theseus_Crommyonian_Sow_Louvre_G637.jpg>.

"The *Syracusia* [Greek ship]." Public Domain. Creative Commons Attribution-Share Alike 3.0 Unported License. <http://creativecommons.org/licenses/by-sa/3.0/deed.en>. *Wikimedia Commons.* 18 May 2011. Web. 28 May 2015. <http://commons.wikimedia.org/wiki/File:The_Syracusia.png>.

"The Fox without a Tail." *The Fables of Aesop.* Trans. Joseph Jacobus. London: Macmillan, 1922. *Wikisource.* <*http://en.wikisource.org/wiki/The_Fables_of_%C3%86sop_(Jacobs)/The_Fox_without_a_Tail*>.

"Duncan Phyfe Chair, 1815." Used with the kind permission of the Stanley Weiss Collection, Providence, RI. n.d. Web. 30 May 2015. <http://www.stanleyweiss.com/>.

"Eighteenth-century Sloops." *Sloop Phyllis*. Creative Commons Attribution-Share Alike 2.0 Generic License.
<http://creativecommons.org/licenses/by-sa/2.0/>. n.d. Web. 28 May 2015.
<http://www.sloopphyllis.com/html/a_short_history_.html>.

Chapter 4, Writing a Good Paragraph

"Little Angel [girl praying]." Nikoreto. *Flikr*. Creative Commons Attribution-Share Alike 2.0 License.
<https://creativecommons.org/licenses/by-sa/2.0/>. 17 May 2007. Web. 29 May 2015.
<https://www.flickr.com/photos/bellatrix6/1254524551/>.

"Basketball." *I Engage at BCS: Basketball 4 Beginners*. *Wikispaces*. Creative Commons Atttribution-Share Alike 3.0 License.
<http://creativecommons.org/licenses/by-sa/3.0/>. n.d. Web. 29 May 2015.
<https://iengageatbcs.wikispaces.com/Basketball_4_Beginners>.

"Die Schiffe de Columbus [The Ships of Columbus]." Gustav Adolph Closs. PD-US. *Wikimedia Commons*. 7 Jan. 2009. Web. 29 May 2015. <http://commons.wikimedia.org/wiki/File:Gustav_Adolf_Closs_-_Die_Schiffe_des_Columbus_-_1892.jpg>.

"Lacrosse Sticks." *La Escuela*. *Wikispaces Classroom*. Creative Commons Atttribution-Share Alike 3.0 License.
<http://creativecommons.org/licenses/by-sa/3.0/>. <https://spanish2fa.wikispaces.com/La+Escuela>. 29 Oct. 2008. Web. 29 May 2015.

"Old North Church." E. Macdonald. 1882. Public Domain. *Wikimedia Commons*. 22 Jan. 2007. Web. 29 May 2015.
<http://commons.wikimedia.org/wiki/File:Old_North_Church_Boston_1882.jpg>.

Chapter 5, Proverb and Chreia

"Prisse Papyrus." Public Domain. *Wikimedia Commons*. 31 Dec. 2004. Web. 29 May 2015.
<http://commons.wikimedia.org/wiki/File:Prisse_papyrus.jpg>.

"Plato and Aristotle." Public Domain. *Wikimedia Commons*. 13 Mar. 2005. Web. 29 May 2015.
<http://commons.wikimedia.org/wiki/File:Sanzio_01_Plato_Aristotle.jpg>.

"George Washington and the Cherry Tree." PD-US. *Wikimedia Commons*. 26 Aug. 2011. Web. 29 Aug. 2015.
<http://commons.wikimedia.org/wiki/File:Augustine%26George_Washington.jpg>.

"The Good Samaritan." PD-Art. Creative Commons Attribution-ShareAlike 3.0 Unported License.
<http://creativecommons.org/licenses/by-sa/3.0/>. *Wikimedia Commons*. 17 Oct. 2005. Web. 29 May 2015.
<http://en.wikipedia.org/wiki/File:Samaritan.jpg>.

"General Nathanael Greene at Stanton Park." David King. Creative Commons Attribution 2.0 Generic.
<https://creativecommons.org/licenses/by/2.0/>. *Flikr*. 21 Feb. 2010. Web. 3 June 2015.
<https://www.flickr.com/photos/bootbearwdc/4377292926/>.

"Buste de Gaspard de Coligny devant la mairie de Châtillon-Coligny." Public Domain. Wikimedia Commons. 29 Dec. 2008. Web. 3 June 2015. <http://commons.wikimedia.org/wiki/File:Ch%C3%A2tillon-Coligny_-_03.jpg>.

"Captain Smith Saved by Pocahontas." Public Domain. *Wikimedia Commons*. 19 Aug. 2014. Web. 30 May 2015. <http://commons.wikimedia.org/wiki/File:FYFE(1863)_p053_CAPTAIN_SMITH_SAVED_BY_POCHAHONTAS.jpg>.

"Jan Wijnants - Parable of the Good Samaritan." Jan Wijnants. <http://www.hermitagemuseum.org/wps/portal/hermitage/digital-collection/01.+Paintings/46144>. Licensed under Public Domain via *Wikimedia Commons*.
<http://commons.wikimedia.org/wiki/File:Jan_Wijnants_-_Parable_of_the_Good_Samaritan.jpg#/media/File:Jan_Wijnants_-_Parable_of_the_Good_Samaritan.jpg>.

"L'Enfant Plan [of Washington, DC]." Andrew Ellicott. Revised from Pierre (Peter) Charles L'Enfant; Thackara & Vallance sc, Philadelphia 1792. Library of Congress. Licensed under Public Domain via *Wikimedia Commons*.
<http://commons.wikimedia.org/wiki/File:L%27Enfant_plan.jpg#/media/File:L%27Enfant_plan.jpg>.

Chapter 6, Encomium and Invective

" Gr70." par I, Papadimitriou4. Sous licence CC BY-SA 3.0 via *Wikimedia Commons*. <http://creativecommons.org/licenses/by-sa/3.0/deed.en>. 25 June 2007. Web. 30 May 2015. <http://commons.wikimedia.org/wiki/File:Gr70.jpg#/media/File:Gr70.jpg>.

"Betsy Ross making the first flag, 1776 (according to legend)." Copy of painting attributed to Frank McKernan., ca. 1900 - - NARA – 530982" by Unknown or not provided. U.S. National Archives and Records Administration. Licensed under Public Domain via *Wikimedia Commons*. <http://commons.wikimedia.org/wiki/
File:Betsy_Ross_making_the_first_flag,_1776_(according_to_legend)._Copy_of_painting_attributed_to_Frank_McKernan.,_ca._1900_-_-_NARA_-_530982.tif#/media/
File:Betsy_Ross_making_the_first_flag,_1776_(according_to_legend)._Copy_of_painting_attributed_to_Frank_McKernan.,_ca._1900_-_-_NARA_-_530982.tif>.

"Anthony Ashley Cooper, 7th Earl of Shaftesbury. Photograph b Wellcome M0010633" by
<http://wellcomeimages.org/indexplus/obf_images/52/22/de193aa9700e583aa1ea261b5c4b.jpgGallery>.
<http://wellcomeimages.org/indexplus/image/M0010633.html>. Licensed under CC BY 4.0 via *Wikimedia Commons*.

<http://creativecommons.org/licenses/by/4.0/deed.en/>.<http://commons.wikimedia.org/wiki/File:Anthony_Ashley_Cooper,_7th_Earl_of_Shaftesbury._Photograph_b_Wellcome_M0010633.jpg#/media/File:Anthony_Ashley_Cooper,_7th_Earl_of_Shaftesbury._Photograph_b_Wellcome_M0010633.jpg>.

"Governor William Bradford." *Plymouth History*. *Wikispaces Classroom*. 2010. Web. 1 June 2015. <http://bmshistory7p8.wikispaces.com/Plymouth+Colony>.

"Allan Ramsay - King George III in coronation robes - Google Art Project." Allan Ramsay - vgGv1tsB1URdhg at Google Cultural Institute, zoom level maximum. Licensed under Public Domain via *Wikimedia Commons*. 5 Jan. 2013. Web. 1 June 2015. <http://commons.wikimedia.org/wiki/File:Allan_Ramsay_-_King_George_III_in_coronation_robes_-_Google_Art_Project.jpg#/media/File:Allan_Ramsay_-_King_George_III_in_coronation_robes_-_Google_Art_Project.jpg>.

"Doeg the Edomite Kills Ahimelech." "No One Is Insignificant, Not Even Doeg." *That Which We Have Heard and Known*. 19 July 2013. Web. 1 June 2015. <http://thefunstons.com/?p=5695>.

"Appleton's Benedict Arnold." Public Domain. *Wikimedia Commons*. 26 Dec. 2009. Web. 1 June 2015. <http://commons.wikimedia.org/wiki/File:Appletons%27_Arnold_Benedict.jpg>.

Death of Saul. Gustave Doré. Public Domain. *Wikimedia Commons*. 26 June 2010. Web. 1 June 2015. <http://commons.wikimedia.org/wiki/File:076.The_Death_of_Saul.jpg>.

"Benito Mussolini." *AHII Period7*. *Wikispaces Classroom*. n.d. Web. 3 June 2015. <http://ahiiperiod7.wikispaces.com/Italy+1920-1930/>.

Chapter 7, Refutation and Confirmation

"Map by Nicolo Zeno 1558." Licensed under Public Domain via *Wikimedia Commons*. 11 May 2007. Web. 16 June 2015. <https://commons.wikimedia.org/wiki/File:Map_by_nicolo_zeno_1558.jpg#/media/File:Map_by_nicolo_zeno_1558.jpg>

"Mark Twain, Brady-Handy photo portrait, Feb 7, 1871, cropped." Mathew Brady. This image is available from the United States Library of Congress's Prints and Photographs division under the digital ID cwpbh.04761. Licensed under Public Domain via *Wikimedia Commons*. 27 Oct 2007. Web. 16 June 2015. <https://commons.wikimedia.org/wiki/File:Mark_Twain,_Brady-Handy_photo_portrait,_Feb_7,_1871,_cropped.jpg#/media/File:Mark_Twain,_Brady-Handy_photo_portrait,_Feb_7,_1871,_cropped.jpg>

"Injun Joe's Two Victims." PD-1923. *Wikimedia Commons*. 10 June 2009. Web. 16 June 2015. <https://commons.wikimedia.org/wiki/File:Tom_Sawyer_-_11-103.jpg>

Chapter 8, Commonplace

"Pinocchio and Gepetto." PD-US. *Wikimedia Commons*. 1 Mar. 2011. Web. 1 June 2015. <http://commons.wikimedia.org/wiki/File:Le_avventure_di_Pinocchio-pag047.jpg>.

"Illuminated.bible.arp." Adrian Pingstone (User:Arpingstone). Own work. Licensed under Public Domain via *Wikimedia Commons*. 19 Feb. 2005. Web. 1 June 2015. <http://commons.wikimedia.org/wiki/File:Illuminated.bible.arp.jpg#/media/File:Illuminated.bible.arp.jpg>.

Chapter 9, Comparison

"Cinderella and Stepsisters." *Old Book Art*. Creative Commons Attribution-Share Alike 3.0 United States License. <http://creativecommons.org/licenses/by-sa/3.0/us/>. n.d. Web. 1 June 2015. <http://www.gallery.oldbookart.com/main.php?g2_itemId=13902>.

"Christian Enters the Wicket Gate." PD-1923. *Wikimedia Commons*. 19 Nov. 2006 Web. 1 June 2015. <http://commons.wikimedia.org/wiki/File:Pilgrim%27s_Progress_2.JPG>.

"Tipi01." Karl Bodmer (1809-1893). Watercolor on paper by Karl Bodmer from his travel to the U.S. 1832-1834. PD-US. Licensed under Public Domain via *Wikimedia Commons*. 5 July 2007. Web. 1 June 2015. <http://commons.wikimedia.org/wiki/File:Tipi01.jpg#/media/File:Tipi01.jpg>.

"Wampanoag Wetu." Creative Commons Attribution Share-Alike 3.0 License. *Green Period 6-7*. *Wikispaces Classroom*. n.d. Web. 1 June 2015. <http://greenperiod6-7.wikispaces.com/Eastern+Woodlands>.

"Landing-Bacon." Henry A. Bacon. <http://upload.wikimedia.org/wikipedia/commons/f/ff/Panoramic_Boston.jpg.> PD-US. Licensed under Public Domain via *Wikimedia Commons*. 29 July 2007. Web. 1 June 2015. <http://commons.wikimedia.org/wiki/File:Landing-Bacon.PNG#/media/File:Landing-Bacon.PNGArmenian king>.

"Alexander II of Russia photo." Неизвстен. PD-1923. <http://www.runivers.ru/gal/gallery-all.php?SECTION_ID=7085&ELEMENT_ID=460860>. Licensed under Public Domain via *Wikimedia Commons*. 8 Oct. 2013. Web. 1 June 2015. <http://commons.wikimedia.org/wiki/File:Alexander_II_of_Russia_photo.jpg#/media/File:Alexander_II_of_Russia_photo.jpg>.

"Alexander III." Paukrus. Creative Commons Attribution-Share Alike License 2.0 Generic. <https://creativecommons.org/licenses/by-sa/2.0/>. *Flikr*. 31 Oct. 2009. Web. 1 June 2015. <https://www.flickr.com/photos/paukrus/4059773155/>.

Chapter 10, Speech-in-Character

"Loaded Camel." *SWAR*. Creative Commons Attribution-Share Alike 3.0 Unported. <http://creativecommons.org/licenses/by-sa/3.0/>. n.d. Web. 1 June 2015. <http://www.swar.info/2010/11/camel-coloring.html>.

"Robb Harwood as Captain Hook." Public Domain. *Wikipedia*. 30 May 2007. Web. 1 June 2015.
    <http://en.wikipedia.org/wiki/File:DuMaurier.jpg>.
"Charles Dickens 3." enwiki. Licensed under Public Domain via *Wikimedia Commons*. 18 May 2006. Web. 1 June 2015.
    <http://commons.wikimedia.org/wiki/File:Charles_Dickens_3.jpg#/media/File:Charles_Dickens_3.jpg>.